43 Tables

An Internet Community Cooks During Quarantine

43 Tables

An Internet Community Cooks During Quarantine

edited by Kat Robinson

TONTI
PRESS

Published by Tonti Press
Little Rock, Arkansas

All photography by original cooks
with additional images provided by Kat Robinson.

First published October 2020

Manufactured in the United States of America
ISBN 978-1-952547-99-7

Library of Congress Control Number: 2020948389

Notice: The information in this book is true and complete
to the best of our knowledge. It is offered without
guarantee on the part of the editor. The editor
disclaims all liability in connection with the use of this book.

The editor accepted no compensation for inclusion of any element
in this book. All photographs of food consist of edible, real food
not enhanced with photographic tricks, manipulation or fakery,
and are provided by the recipe submitters.

To our home cooks, professional chefs,
amateur bakers, grill masters, and all the
creative and wonderful individuals
who have made these recipes.

To their families and friends,
who have shared in these repasts.

And to the restaurant professionals
whose eateries we haven't been able to enjoy
during this global pandemic.
Hang in there. We will be back.

TABLE OF CONTENTS

FOREWORD

March 13th was the end of the way of life the way we'd known it.

That was the day everything shut down here, there, everywhere in the United States. I'd picked up my daughter from school the day before, thinking she was just getting an extra week of Spring Break. This would be handled quickly, right?

But my daughter didn't go back to school. None of the daughters or sons of my friends did. And many of my friends didn't go back to work for a long time. Some started working remotely. Here, seven months later, some continue to do so.

The shock of it was hard. For me, it meant losing every speaking engagement, every festival appearance, every book signing, every single event I was booked at... within a week. The spring I'd planned was gone. The television special carefully planned to be shot over eight months, evaporated. I went from selling hundreds of books each month, to selling four over the course of three months.

I was far from the only person affected. Friends who had worked in health care continued to go in to work each day, endangering their lives to save others. Folks who lost their jobs in all sorts of fields, found themselves scrambling, taking jobs delivering food and working in grocery stores. Parents who had carefully built lives for themselves and their children found themselves tossed into the roles of educators and teacher's aides, trying to figure out how to Zoom or even what Zoom meant, not only for their own jobs but for kids who had never experienced that level of screen time in their lives.

The news became ominous. Times were dark. No one knew what the future would hold. Was it okay to go see friends? Go shopping? Travel? No one really knew for certain. Most of us were practicing different levels of self-isolation, self-protection and quarantine, seeing ourselves within the walls of our own homes and trying to figure out our best way into a better place.

We were all looking for some sort of light. And we found it. It just happened, in many cases, to be the oven light.

I noticed it first across Facebook, while making a daily attempt to reach out and see how people were doing, trying to catch up with the happenings and goings on that had been shifted, somehow, to virtual events. Grumblings over learning to cook again, or that an ingredient was hard to find, gave way to loaves of fresh baked bread, hearty stews, and roasted turkeys pulled from freezer depths. Social media, once overcome with shots of plates at fine restaurants and diner dives, now blossomed as a community began to make its own dinner. Our collective cooking school, whether from individuals who grew up in the TV dinner age or people who lived on take-out, was in session. Each and every day, home cooks and restaurant chefs were sharing what they were making for their families or themselves, letting us in to visually dine together.

With the shuttering of restaurant dining rooms, my lead game as a restaurant writer and photographer was on indefinite hiatus. But these new views, from the kitchens of so many of those folks who are closest via email and Facebook, inspired me.

The course of this year turned, harshly. But it did come with opportunity. I relished the time I was able to spend with my daughter. The agritourism show I had planned was replaced with something I'd never heard of before this year - a no-contact television program, where I sat up a TV studio in a kitchen by myself, put on a little makeup and my hat and set to cooking in front of cameras normally used to shoot still images, making my own cues and sharing a few recipes. Several of my friends did, too, and we came up with a show with Arkansas PBS, Home Cooking with Kat and Friends, and put it on the air the first week of June.

The interest was there. The idea germinated. The folks sharing their lives and their recipes and a spot at their tables with the world weren't just chefs and restaurateurs but folks from all walks of life. The recipes were widely varied, some quite difficult and some rather easy. They were our best, tastiest efforts, derived from our own experiences and curated around available ingredients. They were innovative and a call-back, too, to other years when we ate most of our meals at home. We had time to cook. And food was something we could celebrate and enjoy, even as the companionship we so crave to share it in, had to be from a distance.

Inspired by the old church and community cookbooks I collect and study, I called out to my friends on Facebook to send me their recipes and photos of what they were cooking for their families. Together, 43 of us sat down together, our collective tables bearing the fruit of our efforts, and came up with what you'll see here. Many are from close by here in Little Rock. Quite a few are from my restaurant community in Arkansas. And more still come from my chosen community, friends who share membership in the Society for Creative Anachronism.

Each photo here, every recipe here, was something we cooked during this pandemic. Most, if not all, were shot on cell phones of various quality. They're the work of the people who made the food. They're honest and authentic, a snapshot of all the things we've been doing while waiting to see what's next, a moment in our own culinary histories.

In-between, you'll find a few photos from life taken during this time, between March and July 2020, showing some of the oddities and moments of everyday life. At the back, there's a place for you to put in your recipe, too.

Better days are ahead. For now, come sit down at the table, our 43 tables, and enjoy a bite - whether it's with the eyes or from your kitchen.

Kat Robinson
Little Rock, Arkansas
October 2020

Appetizers

The day the announcement came that the schools were closing, the stores were hit. The surrealness of what was happening didn't strike me until a visit to Kroger on March 13, 2020 - to find that the staple items were already wiped out. There was a guy playing "Hallelujah" on the violin in the parking lot, and the streets were empty during rush hour on a Friday afternoon.

FRIED GREEN TOMATOES

Ken Dempsey - Sherwood, Arkansas

Green tomatoes
Salt and pepper to taste
2 cups flour
4 eggs
1/2 cup milk
3-4 cups crushed pork rinds

1 1/2 teaspoons Cajun seasoning
Vegetable oil for frying
Shrimp strawberry pico (see recipe)
Remoulade (see recipe)
Chopped cilantro or green onion

Heat vegetable oil to 350°.

Whisk together eggs and milk. Crush pork rinds and blend with Cajun seasoning. Set up a station with bowls of flour, egg wash and pork rind for dipping tomatoes.

Slice tomatoes into 1/4"-1/2" thick slices. Salt and pepper. Lightly dust each tomato in the flour, shaking off any excess. Next, submerge tomato into egg wash. Then, dredge in pork rinds, making sure the tomato is fully covered.

Carefully place tomato slices into hot oil a couple at a time. Fry until golden brown.

To serve, top tomatoes with pico, remoulade, and cilantro or green onion.

Shrimp Strawberry Pico

1 pound cooked & chopped shrimp
1 cup diced grape tomatoes
1/4 cup small red onion, diced
1 1/2 cups fresh raw corn, rinsed
1 1/2 cup ripe strawberries, diced

1 avocado, diced
1 Tablespoon lime juice
1/4 teaspoon kosher salt
1/4 teaspoon course pepper

Gently mix ingredients in large bowl. This makes a large amount, perfect for eating with your favorite tortilla chips after topping your fried green tomatoes.

Remoulade

1/2 cup Duke's mayo
1 Tablespoon lemon juice
1 Tablespoon sugar
1/2 Tablespoon paprika

1 teaspoon hot sauce
1 teaspoon Cajun seasoning
1 Tablespoon mustard

Mix well. Serve as drizzle or for dipping.

BISQUICK™ AND SAUSAGE PINWHEELS

Lillian Eaves - Memphis, Tennessee

2 1/4 cups of dry Bisquick™ baking mix
2/3 cup milk
1 pound sausage (pork, beef, or any other type of sausage will work for this recipe)

Preheat oven to 450 degrees.

Mix baking mix and milk in a bowl until a ball of dough is formed. Relocate the dough ball to a sheet of parchment paper and roll out to a large square or rectangle (*Note: the thinner the dough is rolled, the smaller the resulting pinwheels*).

Once dough is rolled to desired thickness, spread the uncooked sausage thinly and carefully roll the dough into a cylinder. Carefully slice the cylinder into half inch coins. Lay out on a parchment paper lined baking sheet, and bake for 10-12 minutes or until golden brown.

Depending on how thinly you roll the dough and spread or crumble the sausage, this can yield pinwheels ranging from the size of a quarter to several

CHIQUITO STYLE CHEESE DIP
Kat Robinson - Little Rock, Arkansas

1 stick (8 Tablespoons) butter
4 Tablespoons all purpose flour
1 teaspoon paprika
1 teaspoon chili powder
1 teaspoon cumin
1 teaspoon garlic powder
1 teaspoon cayenne pepper
　or Creole seasoning
1 teaspoon hot pepper sauce
½ teaspoon dry mustard
¼ teaspoon salt
2 cups whole milk
1 pound American cheese,
　cubed or sliced

Melt butter in saucepan. Add flour and stir
until flour loses its raw taste, about three minutes.

Add spices and pepper sauce, stirring constantly.

Add cheese and continue to stir until the cheese is melted and completely
incorporated into the emulsion. Remove from heat.

Serve with tortilla or potato chips.

MARY BROWN'S POTATO SALAD
Eric Brown - Peachtree Corners, Georgia

2 pounds of potatoes cut into ¾" cubes (may be peeled or not)
3 hard cooked eggs (or two) chopped
2 or 3 stalks of celery chopped
Paprika, salt and pepper
Celery seeds (if you have and like them)

Suggested dressing ingredients

1/2 cup mayonnaise	lemon juice
1/4 cup mustard	1/2 teaspoon salt
2 Tablespoons sweet pickle relish	1/2 teaspoon black pepper
1 Tablespoon pickle relish juice or	1 teaspoon celery seeds (optional)

First make the dressing. I cannot tell you how much to make. You will make it and you may need more or less, but for this amount I'd start off with ½ cup of mayonnaise and ¼ cup of mustard and 2 tablespoons of sweet pickle relish and a tablespoon of pickle relish juice or lemon juice, with a ½ teaspoon of salt and a half teaspoon of black pepper and if you have it a teaspoon of celery seeds. It should look pale yellow (like when you whip egg yolks and sugar to the point of ribbon stage, somewhere between Land O' Lakes butter yellow and Kerry Gold butter yellow), and the taste of it by itself should make your mouth pucker as if you just bit into a lemon. Don't worry, the potatoes mellow that out. Keep that ratio in mind in case you need to make more dressing. Regardless, after it tastes right, throw in the diced celery so you don't forget.

Next hard cook the eggs. Take the eggs and place in a pan of cold water. Slowly bring just up to the boil, turn off the heat and cover the pan for 10 minutes. After ten minutes empty out the boiled water and pour cold tap water on it (I just run the faucet for about a minute). Remove the shell as you will (a mixture of rolling all around to crack the shell then use a teaspoon to break into the skin. Use an egg slicer to slice the eggs one way, then the other so that it's chopped and not slices. Let cool. You will not put these in the salad until the salad is cooled down, so technically you could wait on the slicing and dicing.

Then boil the potatoes thus: Either peel the potatoes or don't (peeled take on more dressing and is a more flavourful salad, unpeeled is nominally less unhealthy) and cut into 3/4" to 1" cubes. Bring 4 quarts of water to the boil and then add a quart cup of salt (or less but add the salt afterwards so the water boils more quickly). Drop the potatoes in the water and boil for 10 minutes and drain. Then put the drained potatoes into your serving bowl then start to spoon the dressing on the potatoes and stir in. The potatoes should look a little over dressed, not soaked, but definitely like "Huh, did I put too much dressing on? I can't tell).

If you did forget to put the celery in the dressing, now is the time to add it to the potato salad. Put this in the refrigerator, uncovered (preferably), for a couple of hours. Then take out of the refrigerator and if you put plastic wrap on top , remove condensation from it, or just throw it away. At this point, mix in the chopped eggs and sprinkle liberally with paprika, sweet is preferable here, but smoked is fine.

Now is when covering the potato salad is acceptable, because this is best served the next day. Also, note, that if the potato salad looked under dressed at this point, you can make a little more dressing and add before you add t he eggs and paprika preferable.

DEVILED EGGS

Eric Brown - Peachtree Corners, Georgia

6 large eggs, hard-cooked
   (see instructions under Mary
   Brown's Potato Salad)
1 heaped Tablespoon mayonnaise

Some salt and pepper
1 tsp mustard (if you have it)
1 ½ tsp pickle relish
A lot of paprika

After peeling the eggs, cut them long ways and scoop the perfectly cooked (since you followed the directions in Mary Brown's Potato Salad) egg yolks in a bowl. Mash up the egg yolks with the mayonnaise, mustard, and pickle relish. Add some salt and pepper and taste. Adjust accordingly (if you put too much salt in, add a little more pickle relish).

Spoon this mixture into the wholes out from which you scooped the perfectly cooked egg yolks.

Place on a deviled egg plate (or a plate that you think will display your master-pieces well), then sprinkle the top of each with Paprika (smoky paprika is good here. You may add a pinch of cayenne if you are daring. You may add a lot to one of the deviled eggs and name it Judas in Hell. Whomever gets this should get a piece of chocolate as a reward because we are the Browns and we reward with chocolate). Decorate with Pimento Cheese Celery Sticks.

PIMENTO CHEESE CELERY STICKS

Eric Brown - Peachtree Corners, Georgia

No, seriously not a recipe unless you don't have Pimento Cheese (if not, chop some cheddar cheese and mix with some mayonnaise and paprika. Add some pimentos or chop a red bell pepper finely and steam in the microwave on a bed of wet paper towels until the diced bell pepper is soft. OK, so cut your celery sticks into 4" boats and put pimento cheese in the middle. Top with pa- if you have any. Add to the center of a deviled egg tray.

ROASTED GRAPES
Vernette Turner - Paris, Arkansas

We went to Post Winery, who opened their Vineyards to the public because of COVID-19 and them having a bumper crop. We picked a bunch of grapes and one of the people there said to wash them and freeze them until you could use them. So, I was trying to find an easy way to use grapes that wasn't making jelly. In the pictures, I used Red and Bronze Muscadine grapes.

4 cups grapes
2 Tablespoons extra virgin olive oil
2 Tablespoons balsamic vinegar
2 sprigs fresh rosemary

Slice the seeds in half. Remove seeds if grapes have them.

Preheat oven to 425 degrees.

Put grapes in bowl. Pour on oil, vinegar and rosemary. Toss or mix gently to combine.

Put on cookie sheet spread out in single layer. I usually put tin foil on sheet. Bake in oven for 25 minutes.

These are great as a side dish, a wonderful garnish over chicken or pork. I have even eaten them as a dessert.

SPIN ART
(SPINACH ARTICHOKE DIP)
Heather Mbaye - Carrollton, Georgia

4 ounces cream cheese, well softened
2 Tablespoons sour cream
2 Tablespoons mayonnaise
heaping ¼ teaspoon of minced garlic *or* one large clove, chopped fine
heaping ½ cup Italian shredded cheese, plus 2-3 Tablespoons for the top
Black or white pepper, to taste
½ of a 14 ounce can of artichoke hearts
3 ounces frozen chopped spinach, thawed

Preheat oven to 350 degrees. Spray a small (1 quart) baking dish with non-stick cooking spray.

In a mixing bowl, stir together cream cheese, sour cream, mayonnaise, garlic, and pepper.

Drain the artichokes. Separate about ½ the can, and squeeze them to remove as much liquid as possible. Chop finely. Squeeze spinach.

Fold the shredded cheese, chopped artichokes, and spinach into the cream cheese mixture.

Spread mixture evenly into prepared baking dish. Sprinkle the top with a little extra Italian cheese. Bake in preheated oven until heated through and melty, about 20 minutes.

Serve warm with tortilla chips, crackers, or toasted baguette slices. Try it on a toasted bagel for a breakfast treat!

SUGAR COCOA CINNAMON POPCORN

Gigi Coulson - New Orleans, Louisiana

1/4 cup popcorn kernels
1 Tablespoon olive oil (optional)
1 1/2 Tablespoons sugar
1 1/2 Tablespoons cocoa powder

1/4 teaspoon cinnamon
1/4 teaspoon salt
1 Tablespoon melted butter

Mix sugar, cocoa powder, cinnamon, and salt in a small bowl and set aside.

Pop the popcorn by one of two methods:

1. Add the oil to a pot with a couple kernels and put the lid on. Turn heat on high. When the kernels begin to pop quickly pour in the remaining kernels and replace the lid. Shake the pan from side to side. When the popping slows down turn off the heat and pour the popcorn in a bowl
-OR-
2. Add the popcorn to a brown paper lunch bag. Double fold the top. Put in the microwave on popcorn setting. Let cook until pops are 3 seconds apart.

Pour cooked popcorn into a large bowl.

In a small bowl heat the butter int he microwave in 15 second increments until melted. Sprinkle on the popcorn, coating evenly. Now sprinkle the sugar, cocoa, cinnamon mixture over the buttered popcorn while stirring it around. Enjoy!

KITCHEN S'MORES

Hunter Robinson - Little Rock, Arkansas

2 Hershey's chocolate bars (the ones with the sections) or 12 Kisses
12 large marshmallows
24 graham cracker squares (12 four part crackers)
Wooden or metal skewers
Gas stove burner or other stationary fire source

Unwrap chocolate bars. Break into sections (24 total sections).

Place 12 graham cracker squares on flat plate or cutting board. Top each one with two sections of Hershey's chocolate or one Kiss. Have remaining 12 graham cracker squares ready.

Skewer a marshmallow. Over a gas oven or other flame, gently roast the marshmallow, taking care not to set it on fire (or set it on fire, if you like your s'mores burny). Heat until gooey, when the marshmallow starts to slide on the stick. Immediately remove from heat and place on top of the chocolate on one graham cracker square. Mash a graham cracker square on top of the marshmallow, and slide out the skewer.

Repeat until all s'mores   are made. Makes 12. Serving size depends on   the individual.

BUFFALO WINGS
Heather Mbaye - Carrollton, Georgia

Approximately 20 wing portions, frozen or fresh
4 Tablespoons butter
1 cup Frank's Red Hot Sauce.
Cayenne pepper (optional)
ranch dressing (optional)

Place frozen or fresh wings in an instant pot. Cook on high pressure for about 8 minuets if frozen; 5 if fresh. Alternately, cook fresh or thawed wings in a steamer for 12 minutes.

While they are cooking, melt butter in a saucepan at low to medium heat. Do not allow to separate or brown. Pour butter into a heat safe bowl, add Frank's red hot sauce. (This will make a mild to medium wing; for a hotter wing sauce, add 1/4 teaspoon of cayenne at a time until it's at the desired heat.

Remove wings from steamer. Toss wings in about half the sauce. Cook in a 425 degree oven for 15-20 minutes until crisp. Serve with the remaining sauce as a dip, or pour remaining sauce on the wings while still hot and serve with ranch style dressing.

SAMOSAS
Rebecca McGraw - Conway, Arkansas

Here's a nice recipe you can do with some things probably already in your pantry. Plan ahead; it takes time to execute. Also there are no measurements...if you're the sort of cook who needs measurements I'm sorry. Try winging this one though; it's hard to mess it up.

So: what we have here are samosa hand pies. First, collect the saddest potatoes you own, the ones starting to turn green and sprout a bit. Peel them and dice til you have a good two or three handfuls, and put them into a pan of salted boiling water and then go back to your project and forget about them. Oops. They're soft. Turn off the heat and to the pot add one peeled chopped carrot, and a third veggie of some sort...I used half a zucchini, chopped, but leftover cooked cauliflower would be good, or a handful of frozen English peas. Stir them in and let them sit in the hot cooking water for a bit. You've got other things to do right now.

Later, a couple of hours before suppertime, dice half an onion and sauté in a skillet with some olive oil and salt till soft. Move the potato-veg mixture into the skillet (save the cooking water). Season with salt, pepper, cumin (add more, that's not enough), turmeric and curry powder. Stir till it's well-mixed and you can smell the spices cooking. Smush it all up with the spatula, add some potato water if it's looking dry, and let it sit and cool for at least a half-hour. An hour is better, probably.

To make the pastry, dump some flour in a bowl (a cup or two), add some melted butter (I used maybe two tablespoons...it was the end of the stick. Or use margarine or Crisco to be vegan) and stir, then add enough of the remaining potato-cooking water a little bit at a time till it forms a soft dough. Don't get out the mixer, just do this with a fork and your hands. Pinch off balls of dough and pat them flat with your hand. Fill with the spiced potato-veg mixture, fold over, and pinch shut, flattening slightly as you do.

Fry till golden in a bit of vegetable oil. Drain on paper towels or, if you're running low, a bit of brown paper sack will do. Or you might try baking them, I dunno. I don't think the pastry would be quite so flaky if you did though.

This dipping sauce is a bit of garlic jam mixed with apple butter and a splash of cider vinegar. John and I are suckers for preserves, and we have maybe 30 jars of various jams and jellies collected from various farmers markets that need to be removed from the pantry and eaten. Now is as good a time as any!

This all sounds incredibly complicated, but I assure you it wasn't. Making the filling is the most time-consuming part but mainly because you have to wait on the veggies to cook (twice) and then cool.

BANANA, PEANUT BUTTER and MAYO POPSICKLES

Christy Seelye-King - Atlanta, Georgia

This flavor combination is the basis for a favorite Southern delicacy in sandwich form, and it makes such a great popsickle too! Perfect for an afternoon snack!

2 ½ cups chopped frozen banana
1/3 cup peanut butter
2 ½ tbsp. Duke's Mayonnaise

Peel and freeze the bananas. (The bananas are sweetest when the peels start to turn brown.) While frozen, dice them into ½" chunks. Keep frozen until ready to assemble.

Line a shallow plastic container with plastic wrap. Spread the peanut butter in a thin layer over the bottom and freeze. When the peanut butter has firmed up in the freezer, remove the plastic wrap with the disc of frozen PB and cut into small dice. Creating small, frozen chunks of the peanut butter will allow the chunks to stay separate from the bananas and provide tasty bursts of flavor.

Combine the frozen banana chunks and small diced peanut butter into a bowl. Toss with the mayonnaise. The mayo will add some creaminess, tartness and salt, and hold the banana and peanut butter chunks together.

Press into popsickle molds. Freeze until firm.

Soups and Salads

Grocery stores were considered essential; even so, many of us were concerned about surfaces possibly being contaminated with the virus. We stowed stuff back in our pantry, cut down or eliminated trips to the store, and started using delivery services. Toilet paper, bleach, rubbing alcohol, and cleaning supplies became scarce, while beef and other staples became far more expensive.

DUMP TRUCK CHILI
Vernette Turner - Paris, Arkansas

1 pound ground beef
1-2 cups Minute Rice
1 package McCormick chili seasoning
1 large can tomato sauce
   or 1 regular can tomato sauce and
    1 regular can diced tomatoes
1 can chili beans
1 can corn

Brown your hamburger meat.

Boil 3 cups water and add rice when it boils.

Dump all cans of ingredients in the water and rice. Mix together. Let it heat up again.

Add hamburger to the chili mixture.

You can top with cheese and sour cream if you wish.

Easy recipe of dumping cans together and making something yummy!
~ V

DEER AND BARLEY STEW
Remington McNew - Cleveland, Arkansas

2 Tablespoons olive oil
1 pound cubed deer meat
1 garlic clove diced
1 celery stalk top, chopped
1 yellow onion, chopped
3 potatoes, peeled and chopped
2 carrots, peeled and chopped
1 turnip, peeled and chopped

1 bay leaf
Salt and pepper to taste
8 cups beef, turkey, or chicken stock
1 teaspoon Cavender's Greek
    Seasoning
½ teaspoon savory
½ teaspoon marjoram
¾ cup barley

In Dutch oven, brown deer meat in olive oil. Add onions, garlic, and celery. Sauté til tender.

Add stock. Bring to boil before adding all the seasoning and vegetables. Bring to gentle boil. Stir once before putting lid on pot.

Stir often, always replacing lid after. Cook till veggies are tender. Add barley. Cook at gentle boil for 15 more minutes.

Keep warm on the side of the fire until ready to eat. Works well with course bread. This also works with beef.

IRISH STYLE SEAFOOD CHOWDER
Dee Rowe-Garcia - Worcester, Massachusetts

Just like the seafood chowders found in parts of County Clare. Heavenly with brown or soda bread.

2 Tablespoons butter
3 pieces bacon (raw diced)
1/2 onion, diced
1 Tablespoons salt
Pepper

1/2 teaspoon dill
Large bay leaf
24 ounces clam juice or seafood
  stock (we do a bit of both)
3 generous cups potato, cubed small

8 ounces clam meat, rough chop (fresh or frozen)
8 ounces diced scallops or diced shrimp
Roux (4 Tablespoons flour + Tablespoon butter)
1 cup cream
1 cup milk

In large sauce pan, add butter, bacon, onion, salt, pepper and dill. Cook on medium until bacon fat is melted and onions are tender but not browned. Add potatoes, bay leaf and stock/juice. Cook until potatoes are tender. Add seafood. Prep roux in frypan and add to pot, stirring until well mixed and thickened (about 1 min). Add milk and cream, cook until heated.

TACO SOUP

Stephanie Wilson - Houston, Texas

1 large can chicken, or 12-16 oz shredded cooked chicken
1 14 ounce can chicken broth
1 10 ounce can condensed cream of chicken soup
1 10 ounce can green enchilada sauce
1 14 ounce can black beans
1 14 ounce can pinto beans
1 14 ounce can corn
1 14 ounce can diced tomatoes
1 packet taco seasoning

Dump all into pot in no particular order. Heat through; serve with shredded cheese, sour cream and corn chips. Serves 6-8 depending on appetite and serving size.

PANTRY VEGGIE SOUP

Stephanie Wilson - Houston, Texas

1 pound ground beef, ground turkey, or ground pork breakfast sausage
1 onion, diced
2 14 ounce cans mixed vegetables
1 14 ounce can green peas
1 14 ounce can diced potatoes
1 14 ounce can diced tomatoes
1 12 ounce can V-8 juice
Beef bouillon, seasoned salt and/or soy sauce to taste (one or any
    combination will do; be careful not to oversalt)
Pepper to taste

Brown the meat with the diced onions; drain if necessary. Add all canned ingredients and season to taste. Heat through and serve. Makes approximately 6-8 servings depending on appetite and serving size.

TOMATO SOUP
Jessica Page - Oberküps, Germany

> I make this at least once a week it seems, Normally
> I put dumplings in mine. Enjoy.

1 Tablespoon olive oil
1 small onion, chopped
2 cloves garlic, minced
1/2 tsp crushed red pepper flakes (optional but advised)
2 Tablespoons tomato paste
1 Tablespoons fresh thyme (feel free to add other herbs as well)
2-28 ounce cans of whole tomatoes (56 oz total)
2 cups water or stock (I use chicken or veggie)
salt and pepper to taste
1 heavy pinch of sugar (about 1 tsp)

Soften the onions in the oil. Add garlic and pepper flakes. Add the tomato paste. Cook until the paste is a deep red, 2-3 minutes.

Add water or stock, cook another ten minutes.

Blend with an immersion blender or pulse it in a blender until smooth. Add sugar, then salt and pepper to taste.

Optional: Top with unsweetened whipped cream or blend in a 1/2 c of cream.

GAZPACHO SOUP
Kat Robinson - Little Rock, Arkansas

3 large tomatoes, cubed
3 small cucumber, peeled and cubed
1/2 cup finely chopped onion
1/2 cup finely chopped bell pepper
1/2 teaspoon garlic powder
dash sugar
juice of 1/2 lemon
2 cups tomato juice
1/2 cup light oil
salt and pepper to taste
dash pepper sauce, optional

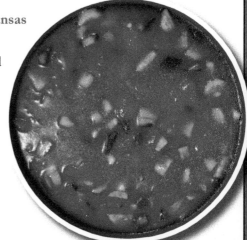

Combine all ingredients and refrigerate at least one hour. Serve in chilled bowls or cups.

BUTTERNUT AND APPLE SOUP
Ruthie Pepler - Harriet, Arkansas

1 whole butternut squash, roasted
  and scooped out
4 apples quartered and roasted,
  then peeled
1 small onion, diced fine
2 cups chicken stock *or* 2 teaspoons
  chicken base and 2 cups water
1 teaspoon grated ginger
  or 1/4 teaspoon ground
1 Tablespoon butter
water to cover
1/4-1/2 cup yogurt or cream to
finish

In a 4 quart Dutch oven, sauté onions in butter until soft. Add roasted butternut and apples (if using fresh diced apple sauté with onions). Add ginger and stir.

Add chicken stock and additional water. Bring to a boil and reduce to a simmer. Cook 15-20 minutes.

Cool slightly and purée if desired. Stir in cream or yogurt or both!

Serve immediately or if making for later cool and refrigerate.

THE AWESOME SOUP
Heather Mbaye - Carrollton, Georgia

> Once upon a time we were iced in in Atlanta and wanted soup. With what we had on hand, this is what came out. I didn't name it – my friend did when she asked me to make more of "the awesome soup with the chicken and potatoes."

2 cups cooked chicken	Teaspoon ground thyme
5 cups chicken broth	half a cup of heavy cream
3 cups cubed potatoes	*For the roux:*
1 1/2 Tablespoon ground cumin	2.5 Tablespoons unsalted butter
Half a teaspoon white pepper	3 Tablespoons all-purpose flour

Chop or shred two cups cooked chicken. This can be boiled, baked, or even rotisserie, but avoid heavily seasoned chicken. Peel and cube about 3 cups of potatoes.

Put chicken and broth in a 5 quart pot. Bring to a boil; add potatoes, cumin, white pepper, thyme. Cook for about 10 minutes on high at a rolling boil with no lid. While this is happening, start your roux (below). Add heavy cream; return to a boil and cook until the potatoes are done through. You are reducing the liquid, so be sure to leave the lid off. Add roux, boil for about 5 minutes. Remove from heat and allow to thicken.

For the roux
In a small non-stick pan, melt butter. Do not allow the butter to brown or separate. Add the flour. Cook on medium to medium high, stirring constantly until a rich caramel brown is reached. Do not allow the roux to develop black spots.

GRACE'S SOUP
Jerrie Parker

2 pounds hamburger meat,
  browned and drained
2 cans ranch style beans
2 cans hominy, drained

1 small can green chiles, optional
1 large jar picante sauce
1 package dry ranch dressing

Place all ingredients in Crock Pot and cook on slow for three hours.

EASIEST SOUP EVER
Jerrie Parker

1 pound hamburger meat,
  browned and drained
1-10 ounce can Ro-Tel
2-15 ounce can Veg-All

1-10 ounce can minestrone soup
1-15 ounce can whole kernel corn
1-15 ounce can diced tomatoes
1-15 ounce can ranch style beans

Don't drain vegetables! In a large pot, mix all ingredients. Simmer for two hours or make in Crock Pot on low for three hours. Can be made with or without meat.

Sale $ 12.06
Gallons 10.994

The craziest part for me, as a traveler, is having to stop at just the moment the price of gas fell below a dollar in many places.

GRANDMA'S BUTTER BOWL SALAD
Andrea Wilson - Cabot, Arkansas

"This is a treat during the cucumber/tomato season at Pea Farm Bistro. It is named Grandma's Butter Bowl, because that is what our grandmother would store it in the fridge. Basically, it is our take on a Cucumber Tomato Salad. We make large amounts for the bistro."

Cucumbers, peeled and cubed or sliced
Tomatoes, cubed and sliced
Red onion, sliced
Salt and pepper to taste
Sliced peppers (optional)

Dressing
Equal parts apple cider vinegar and sugar, mixed well

Toss vegetables in dressing to coat. Refrigerate for at least six hours.

HYMNAL SALAD FOR FOUR
Eric Brown - Peachtree Corners, Georgia

My family calls it this because I keep this recipe on a piece of paper in my Evangelical Lutheran Worship hymnal.

½ cup chopped walnuts

14 ounce jar of sliced beets drained and chopped
  (OK, If you're not into this, try a half a cup of sliced almonds)

2 large oranges *or* four mandarins, separated

1 head of Cos (romaine) chopped

4 radishes chopped

½ a small red onion sliced (and then put in a freezer bag with the juice of a lime or even just about ¼ cup lime juice from a squeeze bottle. The red onion will turn almost fuchsia and will have a sweet and tangy flavor without the burn of the red onion).

2 ribs of celery, chopped

Salad dressing:

2 Tablespoons cherry preserves (for Easter I went the orange route because that's what Norwegians do at Easter, so I used orange marmalade)

2 Tablespoons vinegar

1 teaspoon poppyseeds (not essential. Want some umph? Try sesame seeds or sunflower)

3 Tablespoons olive oil (good and flavoursome in this instance)

Salt and pepper (and if using orange marmalade, some nutmeg)

Combine all ingredients. Serve.

CORN SALAD
Kat Robinson
- Little Rock, Arkansas

6 ears roasted corn on the
  cob, cut from the ear
3 medium tomatoes, chopped
1 red onion, chopped
1/2 cup fresh basil, chopped
1/2 bottle Italian dressing

Combine all ingredients.
Refrigerate overnight.
Serve cold.

LINCOLN HIGHWAY SALAD DRESSING
David Backlin - Fort Smith, Arkansas

6 ounces tomato soup, undiluted
1 cup vegetable oil
3/4 cup granulated sugar
1 teaspoon garlic salt
1/2 cup cider vinegar
salt and pepper

1 teaspoon paprika
1 teaspoon dry mustard
1 teaspoon Worcestershire sauce

Blend all ingredients in a blender or food processor till smooth. Chill. Will keep in refrigerator for several months.

Trailblazer Diner
Located on Lincoln Highway U. S. Rt. 1
1 mile North of Roosevelt Blvd.
Midway between Philadelphia and Trenton

FRUIT SALAD FOR 4 TO 6
Eric Brown - Peachtree Corners, Georgia

You want about ½ to ¾ of a cup of fruit salad per person. When we had plenty of vegetables in our casserole, I served this as a side. That way we could pretend we were eating this for dessert.

1 large apple cored and diced (2 small will do)

An orange or a couple of mandarins (or if you have tinned mandarin oranges, great)

A banana (or kiwi or stoned cherries or grapes cut in half)

I like dried cherries that have been put in boiling water for 5 to 10 minutes, but other dried fruit would work as well as not any dried fruit at all

Some seeds or nuts (or not)

Sprinkle with some lemon juice or lime juice if you have it (this keeps the fruit from turning brown and brightens the flavor)

Dress with mayonnaise or (because my sister doesn't like mayo) yoghurt (fruit flavoured is great, plain is good too, if Greek, cut with some milk or with more lemon or lime juice.

Vegetables
and Sides

$2 29

When the farmers markets reopened, we fell on them with excitement. Something about the act of self-isolating made the hunger for fresh, locally grown fruits and vegetables even stronger. I found myself frequenting the outdoor facilities of Urbana Farmstead and the Me and McGee Market, looking for produce.

CURLY POTATO CASSEROLE
Susannah Austin - Memphis, Tennessee

So... my mom got me a "Big Boss Slice-aroo" (it makes curly fries, and zoodles). So, I decided to play with some potatoes.

If you cut down one side, it keeps them from spiraling, makes them like hash browns. I spiralized a couple of potatoes, threw them in a big baking dish, added two well blended eggs and some shredded cheese (in this case, it was pepper jack, about 3/4 cup). Mixed that well and set it aside. Browned a pound of ground beef with some seasonings, whatever we had handy... Added a can of cream of potato soup, and some cream of mushroom soup in the fridge. Then I found some leftover peas in the fridge, and a chunk of Velveeta, so I added them, too!

Poured that mixture over the potato/egg layer, and then topped that with fully spiralized potatoes. Stretched them out so they wrapped around each other like ribbons. It made a pretty tall pile of curls on top! (sadly, that pile cooked down, considerably.).

Baked it at 375°F. for 40 minutes.

CRUNCHY SZECHUAN GREEN BEANS

Leif Hassell - Little Rock, Arkansas

2 Tablespoons sesame oil
1 pound green beans, trimmed
2 Tablespoons soy sauce
1 teaspoon fresh ginger, minced
1 teaspoon ground orange peel
1 Tablespoon chili garlic sauce

½ teaspoon szechuan peppercorns
   (whole, ground and sifted)
¼ cup orange juice
1 teaspoon sugar
¼ cup hoisin sauce
toasted sesame seeds, for garnish

Clean and trim your green beans. Set them aside.

Whisk together hoisin, sugar, and orange juice to thin to runny consistency. Set aside.

Heat a wok or large, heavy bottomed pan over high heat. Whisk together your soy sauce, ginger, chili garlic sauce, peppercorns and orange peel and cook for 1 minute or so, until beginning to reduce just a bit. Add in your green beans and cook, stirring often, for 5-7 minutes, until the beans are beginning to blacken in parts and blister. Remove from heat and toss in hoisin sauce mixture.

Serve hot, garnished with sesame seeds. Serves six.

MUSHROOM PASTY
Terri Dutton - Salem, Arkansas

1 quart fresh mushrooms sliced
2 onions, finely chopped
1-2 cloves garlic, finely chopped
1 Tablespoon olive oil

1-2 Tablespoons Worcestershire sauce
Red wine to taste (optional)
1 cup grated hard cheese
Double pie crust

In a skillet, caramelize onions and garlic in olive oil. Add mushrooms, along with Worcestershire sauce and red wine. Cook together with onions until soft and the liquid has been absorbed. Remove from heat and fold in cheese. Set aside.

Heat oven to 350. Lightly oil a pie pan or cookie sheet. Lay half the pie crust down in the pan or sheet. Spoon mushroom filling into the crust, leaving room to seal. Top with remaining crust. Use a fork to seal the edges.

Bake for 30-35 minutes or until crust is nicely browned. Remove from oven and allow to sit for at least 10 minutes before slicing and serving.

3

HOW TO COOK CHICKWEED
(or almost any other type of green)
Melinda LaFevers - Searcy, Arkansas

I learned this method in a foraging class, and have adapted it to almost any type of greens - kale, turnip, spinach, etc.

Collect your greens early in the morning, but after the dew has a chance to dry, if possible. Chickweed can often be found growing around or over old tree stumps, along the edges of buildings, at the base of trees, etc. Wash carefully to remove any dirt and debris, and pick out any grass or plants that should not be included. Remember that greens cook down a lot, so you need more than you think you will for a good serving. I like to collect a plastic grocery bag at least half full if it is just for myself.

In a large skillet or pan, fry up some bacon until crisp (everything good has bacon, right?) How much depends on personal taste. I will use half to a full package.

Remove bacon and place on paper towels to cool and drain.

Healthy: drain off bacon grease and add olive oil to pan.
Don't care: Use bacon grease left from frying the bacon.

Chop up or mince garlic to taste - I like at least a couple of cloves, up to an entire bulb, depending on size of garlic and quantity of greens.

Sauté garlic until soft.

Add chickweed and/or other greens and sauté, stirring frequently to coat all of it with the now garlic flavored oil or bacon grease.

Turn down heat and cover, cooking until desired doneness. Some people like it thoroughly cooked, others only like it wilted - usually only a few minutes.

Crumble up bacon and stir into the greens.

Add a few dashes of malt, balsamic, or apple cider vinegar to taste.

Be sure to bake some cornbread to soak up the pot likker.

SQUASH LIKE MOM'S
Beverly Sanders - Benton, Arkansas

1/2 stick of butter	salt and pepper
4 large squash	dash of sugar
1 Vidalia onion	1/2 cup water

Heat skillet to medium. Add all ingredients and stir. Place lid on skillet. Occasionallly stir. When squash is tender, turn heat to high and let liquid cook off, stirring often. Ready when the squash get a little scorched on the edges.

FRIED SQUASH
Kat Robinson - Little Rock, Arkansas

It's indigenous to Arkansas, it's one of summer's most prolific vegetables, and it's such an easy side dish. This lightly fried squash is a wonderful addition to any lunch or dinner.

3 large squash, sliced 1/4 inch thick	1/2 cup milk
1 cup flour	1 egg
1/4 teaspoon salt	cooking oil
1/4 teaspoon pepper	

Heat 1/2 inch oil in frying pan. Stir together salt and pepper with flour in one bowl. In a second bowl, beat egg, add milk and stir well. Dip each squash slice in egg wash, then into the flour mixture, and immediately drop into the hot oil. Let cook until lightly brown on the bottom, then flip and fry until the other side is brown. Drain on paper towels and serve.

SQUASH CASSEROLE
Teresa Horner - Hot Springs, Arkansas

Squash Casserole is a recipe I came up with several years ago when I had harvested too much squash at one time. During quarantine, my grocery run person purchased more yellow squash than I needed so this recipe popped up again!

1 box Jiffy™ cornbread mix
(during quarantine I made my own cornbread and added extra sugar to make it sweet)

1 teaspoon. dried thyme (or 2 springs of fresh stem removed)

2 chicken bullion cubes

1 large sweet yellow onion chopped

4-5 yellow squash sliced in thick circles (can mix yellow + zucchini if you like)

1 block soften cream cheese

1/2 cup shredded cheddar cheese

2 Tablespoons butter

Milk for Jiffy™ Mix

2 eggs beaten plus Jiffy™ mix

Bake Jiffy™ cornbread according to box directions. Meanwhile, slice squash and chop onions. Once veggies are prepped add them to a pot big enough for them to be covered with 1 inch of water. Add chicken bullion cubes and thyme. Cook until squash is tender. Drain and save cooking liquid. Set aside squash and cooking liquid until cornbread is baked and cooked.

Once cornbread is cooled, crumble it into a large mixing bowl. Add cooked veggies, 2 beaten eggs and both cheeses. Mix all ingredients together, if mixture is stiff add cooking liquid until mixture is soupy (like a cake mix). Pour into a butter baking dish and cake at 350° for 35-45 minutes. This is done once toothpick is inserted in the middle and comes out clean.

SICILIAN POTATO AND GREEN BEAN SALAD
Margie Raimondo - Little Rock, Arkansas

2 pounds small red potatoes	1/2 teaspoon black pepper
1 pound green beans	4 Tablespoons olive oil
2-3 scallions, sliced	3 Tablespoons red wine vinegar
2 Tablespoons fresh basil, chopped	Juice from half of a lemon
1 teaspoon dried oregano	Salt
1/2 teaspoon onion powder	Pinch of sugar
1/2 teaspoon garlic powder	

Cook potatoes in boiling water until tender. Drain the potatoes, rinse with cold water and allow to cool. Cook the green beans in the same manner.

Cut the potatoes into bite-size chunks. Cut the beans into 1-inch pieces.

In a bowl, whisk together all of the remaining ingredients. Add the potatoes and beans and toss gently to coat.

Serve immediately or refrigerate and serve cold. Serves 6-8.

ZUCCHINI AND GOAT CHEESE FETA FRITTERS

Jacinda Gregory - Beebe, Arkansas

> Soft fluffy on the inside and nice and crispy on the outside.
> It's a great way to use all that zucchini.

3-4 whole zucchini ; grated
2 teaspoon salt
3/4 cup crumbled goat cheese feta
2 large eggs ; beaten
3 green onions ; cleaned and thinly
sliced
1/4 cup fresh mint ; finely chopped
1/2 teaspoon black pepper
1 1/2 cups self raising flour
oil ; for frying

Wash the zucchini and cut off the ends leaving the peel on. Grate with box grater or a food processor. You will need about 4-5 cups so judge how much to grate depending on the size of your zucchini. Place your grated zucchini in a colander placed over a large bowl. Sprinkle zucchini with salt and mix so that all pieces are salted. Let drain for about 30 minutes. Gently move the zucchini and press on sides of the colander. Gently squeeze with your hands to remove the water.

While you are waiting on your zucchini to drain, mix together; eggs, green onion, mint, feta cheese and black pepper. Once your zucchini is drained of as much water as you can add this to your wet mixture. Mix in about 1 1/2 cups all purpose flour to create a soft dough. The longer you let it sit the wetter the dough will become because of the extra moisture in the zucchini.

In a pan on the stove add enough oil to submerge your dough balls, and turn on medium high heat. You can also use a deep fryer set to 350 degrees. Place a plate with several paper towels.

Using a teaspoon or a small cookie dough scoop drop dough into the hot oil. Don't over crowd the pan. They need room to move and you also don't want to cool down your oil to fast. Fry them for about 2-3 minutes each, turning them or splashing the tops with hot oil to get an even golden brown color. Remove and place on paper towel lined plate. If you don't want these round like hush puppies, you can place in a shallow frying pan that with just a couple of inches of oil. They will spread out and become flat.

Sever with a tzatziki sauce.

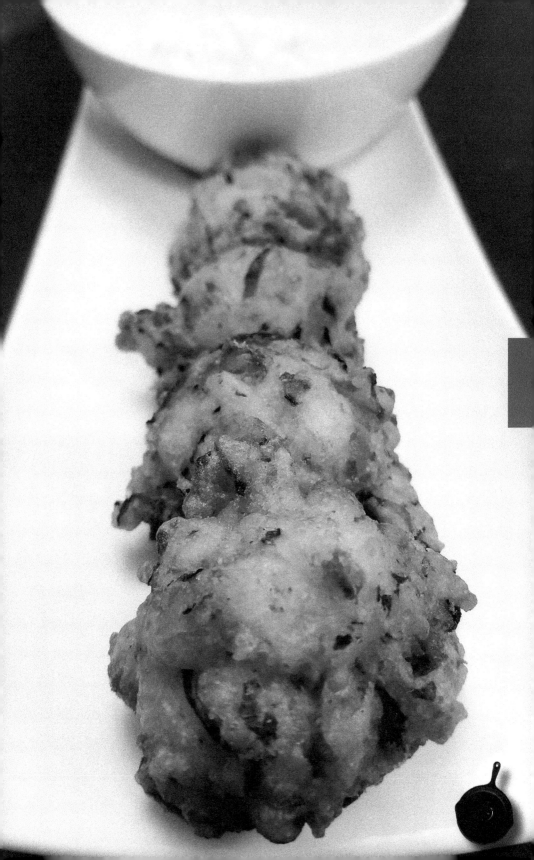

Breads

Our pets started acting strangely a few weeks after the stay at home orders began. For some, it was the first time their humans had ever spent every hour of the day in the house with them. Some relished the time; others acted out, missing their solitude.

POPOVERS
Eric Brown - Peachtree Corners, Georgia

We decided to do a roast dinner and, of course, we had popovers. This recipe can easily be doubled. Also, I did these in regular muffin tins. If you have mini muffin tins, you could make a full dozen instead of six.

2 large eggs at room temperature
175 ml lukewarm milk (that's 175 grams as well)
¼ tsp salt
90 gm all-purpose flour
25 gm butter, melted
muffin tin with at least 6 muffin cups, greased well, including the area between the cups
a toothpick

Heat the oven to 465 and place rack on a low shelf.

Once the oven is heated the 465, whisk the eggs, butter, salt and warm milk together until completely mixed. Whisk in flour and get rid of all big lumps.

Pour into the six muffin cups (or 12 if mini), and immediately place in oven on low shelf. Lower oven temperature to 450 and bake for 20 minutes (do NOT open oven door).

Without opening oven door, lower temperature to 350 and bake for an additional 15 minutes.

Open the oven and quickly prick each muffin once or twice with a toothpick then close the door. This allows the steam in the popovers to release so the insides dry a little. Allow to bake an additional 5 minutes.

Serve immediately.

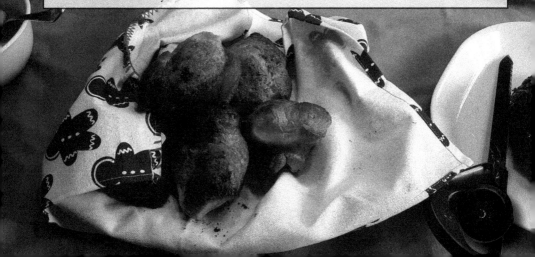

HILDEGARD'S BISCUITS TO BRING JOY
Gigi Coulson - New Orleans, Louisiana

2 teaspoons ground nutmeg
2 teaspoons ground cinnamon
1/2 teaspoon ground clove
2 cups spelt flour

4 Tablespoons honey
water enough to moisten
drizzle of olive oil

Combine all dry ingredients ,then add just enough water and a drizzle of olive oil to bring the mix together into a workable dough. Smear your fingers with olive oil to handle the sticky dough best. Roll the dough out on a floured surface to about 1/2" thickness, place into pie pan and press until it covers the bottom. Score it into triangles.

Bake at 350F for around 15 minutes. Cut and enjoy.

This recipe originated with Hildegard Bingen in the 13th century. She wrote "If a person eats nutmeg it opens up his heart, makes his judgment free from obstruction, and give them a good disposition." I hope it helps you during this pandemic.

SWEET POTATO BISCUITS
Jamie McAfee - Pine Bluff, Arkansas

3/4 cups cooked mashed sweet potato (about one sweet potato)
1/3 to 1/2 cup whole milk as needed
1 1/2 to 2 cups all purpose flour, plus more for dusting (gluten free okay)
2 Tablespoons sugar
1 Tablespoon baking powder
1 teaspoon salt
6 Tablespoons cold, unsalted butter cut into small bits

Preheat oven to 375 degrees. Grease baking sheet with butter, oil or cooking spray. In a small bowl, whisk together sweet potato and milk. Set aside.

In a large bowl, whisk together dry ingredients. Cut butter in with a pastry cutter or fork until the mixture attains a crumbly texture or resembles coarse meal. Add the sweet potato mixture and gently fold to combine. Add the remaining milk a little at a time until all the flour is moistened. The amount of milk you will need will depend on the moisture of the sweet potato.

Sprinkle a small amount of flour on a work station. Turn the dough out onto the surface and kneed lightly 2-3 times with the palm of your hand until the dough comes together. Pat the dough out into a 1/2 inch thick round. Using a 2 1/2 inch biscuit cutter, cut the dough into biscuits. Gently re-roll the scraps and cut out more biscuits.

Place on prepared baking sheet and bake 12-14 minutes or until light golden brown and firm to the touch. Serve warm or at room temperature.

NIDO CINNAMON ROLLS
Heather Mbaye - Carrollton, Georgia

Dough:
1/2 cup warm water
    (110 degrees f/45 degrees c)
2 Tablespoon Nido Kinder
    (sweetened powdered milk*)
1 large egg, room temperature
2.5 Tablespoon unsalted butter, melted
1/2 tsp salt
¼ cup white sugar
1 ¼ teaspoon bread machine yeast
2 ¼ cup bread flour

*Nido Kinder can be replaced with 2 Tablespoons regular powdered milk and 1 teaspoon of sugar, or replace the water AND the Nido with ½ cup warm whole fat milk and 1 teaspoon of white sugar.

Filling:
½ cup brown sugar
¼ Tablespoons cinnamon
2.5 Tablespoons butter, softened

Frosting;
4 ounces cream cheese
¼ cup unsalted butter, softened
½ - ¾ cup confectioner' sugar (taste it after ½ cup as I don't like it quite so sweet as others do!)
½ tsp vanilla extract

Place all ingredients except the flour in a stand mixer with a dough hook in the order indicated by the recipe and mix briefly on low to combine. Add ½ flour. Mix on low until combined (it's not strictly necessary to split the flour but it is less messy). Add remaining flour. Mix on medium high using the dough hoof for 2-3 minutes or until a smooth ball forms.

Turn dough out onto a floured surface. Cover with a clean dish towel and let rest for 10 minutes. Meanwhile, cream brown sugar and cinnamon together, cover; and set aside.

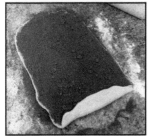

Once dough has rested for 10 minutes, roll out into a 16 x 10 -inch rectangle. Spread dough evenly with 1/3 cup softened butter. Spread cinnamon mixture evenly.

Roll dough up (starting with short edge) tightly; slice (using sharp knife) into 8 rolls approximately 1.25" tall. Place rolls into a medium baking pan. Cover and let rise in a warm place until nearly doubled (about 30-60 minutes, depending on the temperature and humidity in your home).

Note: You can cover and put in refrigerator overnight. They will rise in the refrigerator and this will take a lot of prep time off the next morning. Make sure you let the rolls get to room temperature before you bake them as they will not bake properly from "fridge cold."

Preheat oven to 375 degrees. Bake for 18-20 minutes.

Cream together the butter, cream cheese, and vanilla with a mixer. Add the powdered sugar. Divide evenly; spread over warm rolls.

SWEET ROLLS
Tracy Godsey - Springdale, Arkansas

I've been making sourdough recipes like crazy. My family's favorite are the sourdough sweet rolls. Since we're all stuck together at home, we're eating a lot of family breakfasts and the sweet rolls are a big hit. I've made several kinds of roll in one recipe since everyone has a different favorite.

The standard recipe I started with was the sourdough cinnamon roll recipe on the King Arthur Flour website.

Now for my variations:

Orange rolls: where the cinnamon roll filling calls for brown sugar and cinnamon, use the same amounts of white sugar and orange zest.

Strawberry sweet rolls: Use strawberry jam. *This is my daughter's favorite.*

I will spread all three fillings into the same dough roll (I just put the cinnamon on one third of the roll, the orange on one third and the strawberry on one third). Then slice them to make different flavors of roll in the same batch.

The recipe says to roll up the dough width-wise (short end to short end). I prefer to roll the dough lengthwise (long end to long end). This makes more rolls that are smaller diameter. But as you can see from the picture, even the smaller rolls are pretty big.

My husband is trying to eat vegan for health, so I adapted this recipe for him: instead of egg, I substitute 1/4 cup applesauce. In place of milk, I use plant based milk like soy, almond or coconut milk. In place of butter, I use coconut oil (although there are some very nice vegan butters out there, and butter-flavor Crisco is vegan friendly if you really want that buttery flavor).

Here is a photo of the batch fresh out of the oven. I don't put the icing on myself, since not everyone likes it. Instead I leave it on the side so the kids can sugar up while the adults pretend that they're eating responsibly.

TRADITIONAL IRISH SODA BREAD

Christy Seelye-King - Atlanta, Georgia

4 cups (16 ounces) cake flour
1 teaspoon baking soda
14 ounces buttermilk
1 teaspoon salt

Preheat oven to 425 degrees. Lightly grease and flour a cake pan or baking sheet.

In a large mixing bowl, sift the flour, baking soda and salt. Make a well in the center of the flour mixture and pour in the buttermilk.

Using your fingers, gently bring the dough together. *Do Not Overmix!* The dough should be soft and not too wet or sticky.

Form a round loaf and place on a lightly-floured baking sheet. Take a knife and make two cuts across the top of the loaf in an X shape. Pierce the 4 triangles several times with the knife tip (to let the Irish Fairies out!).

Bake at 425 for 10 minutes, then lower the heat to 400 and bake for 35 more or until the bottom of the loaf sounds hollow when thumped.

Cut into thick slices, smear with butter or jam!

SAVORY BUTTERS FOR ENJOYING WITH BREAD

Kat Robinson - Little Rock, Arkansas

1 pound butter, salted (or one pound unsalted + 1 teaspoon finely ground salt
1 cup any leftover fresh herbs, including the following:

Basil	Sage
Oregano	Parsley
Thyme	Rosemary

4 cloves garlic, finely chopped

Let butter come to room temperature in a medium sized bowl. Place wax paper on a cutting board. Remove any stems from herbs. Place herbs and garlic on board. Cover with wax paper. Smash with rolling pin, bottle bottom or hammer until pulp. Sweep remnants into bowl with butter. Stir and incorporate thoroughly. Press into butter molds or ice cube trays. Freeze. Once frozen, remove portions to plastic bag and store in freezer until day before use. Set out on saucer on counter an hour before ready to serve.

BEER MUFFINS
Kat Robinson - Little Rock

1 16 ounce box Bisquick baking mix
1 12 ounce beer of choice
2/3 cup sugar
1 cup cheese of choice (optional)
Cooking spray

Preheat oven to 350.

Spray a 12 cup muffin plan with cooking spray. Set aside.

Combine Bisquick and sugar in bowl. Add beer and fold with spatula until all Bisquick is incorporated. If using cheese, fold it in gently.

Divide batter between muffin pan cups. Bake at 350 degrees for 18-20 minutes or until tops begin to brown. Serve plain or split with butter.

These muffins are perfect for splitting for a handheld breakfast sandwich with your choice of bacon, Canadian bacon or sausage, egg and the like. This batter can also be used to make 24-36 mini muffins. Cook for 10-15 minutes.

Variations

1. Fold in 1/4 cup bacon bits with 1 cup cheddar cheese.

2. Soak 1/4 cup dried apples in beer 1/2 hour before mixing ingredients. Add 1/2 teaspoon cinnamon and 1/4 teaspoon nutmeg to Bisquick and sugar mix.

3. Add 1/2 cup finely cubed ham and 1/2 cup shredded Swiss cheese.

4. Add 1/2 cup finely chopped broccoli and 1/2 cup American cheese shreds.

5. Reduce beer to 8 ounces and add one can Ro-Tel and 1 cup cubed Velveeta cheese for cheese dip muffins.

6. Before baking, sprinkle 2/3 cups sugar over 1 cup sliced fresh strawberries. Fold with Bisquick mix, then add beer. Omit cheese.

7. Omit cooking spray. Line each muffin with 1 strip bacon. Bake bacon alone for 10 minutes. Remove to paper towels and drain. Drain excess remaining bacon grease from pan. Replace bacon circles in pan. Replace half of sugar with 1/3 cup maple syrup. Bake as directed. When done, split top and add one easy-over egg (optional) before serving.

8. Omit cheese and add 1/2 teaspoon salt. Serve hot with honey and butter.

9. Fold in 1 pound cooked sausage and 1 cup Cheddar cheese into batter. This will increase yield to 18 muffins.

Main Dishes

After a few months cooking at home, people started turning to baking bread, refining their cooking techniques, and in the case of our kitchens, preserving foods. The pandemic took much from us, but it also gave us something unexpected: time.

CHICKEN AND DUMPLINGS

Lillian Eaves, Memphis, Tennessee

In a large pot, cook chicken with mix of carrots, onion, and celery (can add powdered chicken broth or make your own). Season to taste.

In a bowl, sift one cup of all purpose flour and half a teaspoon of salt. Add one capful of vegetable oil, canola works well, and stir with a fork. One tablespoon at a time, add enough ice water to form a ball of dough in the bowl. Cover and let rest for 15 minutes.

Roll out the dough on a floured surface until thin, then cut into smaller pieces with a sharp knife.

Bring the soup to a rolling boil and add the dough pieces to the pot one at a time. Maintain the rolling boil for 15 minutes, stirring gently every five minutes or so (to keep the dumplings from sticking to the bottom of the pot; stirring too often may break up the dough before it has a chance to cook).

Lower heat, and simmer another 10-15 minutes. Serve hot. Wonderful the first day, but even better the next day reheated. This is a family favorite that is also delicious with the addition of fresh garlic, mushrooms, ginger, and garden herbs like basil and rosemary.

PANTRY ARROZ CON POLLO
Chef Cheryl Delong - Bryant, Arkansas

Roast Chicken Thighs

1 pound skin on or boneless
  skinless chicken thighs
1/2 Tabkespoon cumin
1/2 Tablespoon onion powder
1/2 Tablespoon garlic powder

1 Tablespoon chicken bullion powder
2 teaspoons kosher salt
1/2 Tablespoon coarse black pepper
½ cup blended olive oil

Preheat oven to 350 degrees. In a medium mixing bowl add the chicken thighs, oil, and spices then toss to coat. Spread evenly on a baking sheet lined with parchment paper for easy clean up. Using skin on chicken allows the enjoyable texture of crispy skin and is encouraged, turning the pan mid cooking ensures for even cleaning. Timing will vary but 20 to 25 minutes should be enough to cook throughout. The amount of chicken chosen is to allow for a couple thighs per serving.

Beans

3 - 16 ounce cans three bean mixture
  (dark red kidney beans, black
  beans, pinto beans in chili sauce)
1 - 16 ounce can Ro-Tel™ (diced
  tomato, onion, and chili pepper)
1 - 16 ounce can light red kidney beans
1- 16 ounce can black beans

1 medium white onion (diced)
1 Tablespoon cumin
1 Tablespoon onion powder
1 Tablespoon garlic powder
1 Tablespoon kosher salt
1/2 Tablespoon coarse black pepper

This mixture goes into a large stock pan with a heavy bottom, it is as if you are making chili. Use the juices from the pans of the chicken, heat through to 165 degrees about 10 minutes on medium heat.

Cilantro Lime Rice

2 cups Ralston Farms jasmine rice
  or basmati rice
3 limes, juice of
3 1/2 cups water
1 Tablespoon cumin
1 teaspoon onion powder

1 teaspoon garlic powder
1 Tablespoon chicken bullion powder
2 teaspoons salt
½ cup fresh chopped cilantro
3 Tablespoons unsalted butter

Preheat oven to 350 degrees. In a half pan add rice, water, lime juice, butter, and flavorings. Cover with aluminum foil tightly then baked for 45 minutes up to 1 hour until rice is soft.

Remove the foil from rice and stir to fluff grain. Either pour out onto a sheet pan, smoothed out flat to cool or serve immediately..

QUARANTINE CASSOULET
Christy Seelye-King - Atlanta, Georgia

Cassoulet is a traditional French peasant-style dish. It takes simple ingredients and raises them to new heights, and in times of food insecurity, it is a useful recipe to have handy for those dried beans you stocked up in your pantry. Since everyone is spending an extended time at home right now, the long, slow cooking time is also perfectly suited to the times. By allowing the dish to slow-bake it develops layers of deep, rich, golden-brown and delicious colors and flavors, and the kitchen will smell of comfort food the whole time it is in the oven. Save some for later, because this is exactly the kind of dish that gets better the next day!

For the Beans

A variety of beans can be used for this dish. I prefer small white Navy beans, but you could use just about any dried or canned bean you have in the house.

Soak 2 cups of dried white beans. Cover beans with water, cover the bowl with a towel and let them sit out on the counter 8 hours or overnight.

Create a Bouquet Garni pouch with aromatic herbs and spices such as bay leaf, cracked black peppercorn, fresh or dried thyme, roughly chopped garlic, and parsley stems or celery tops. Tie them up in a cheesecloth pouch to cook with the soaked dried beans. If you don't have any cheesecloth, you can put most of the herbs and spices in a tea infuser ball in a pinch and throw it in to cook with the beans.

Drain off the soaking water and discard. (That soaking water now contains a sugar called raffinose, which gives the dried bean its reputation for being 'The Musical Fruit'. Pouring off this non-digestible sugar helps make beans a less gaseous food, which is helpful when you and your family are quarantined together!).

Cover the beans in several inches of fresh water. Do not add salt at this point. Add the Bouquet Garni and cook on a medium heat for 90 minutes or so until the beans are just tender, but are not losing their shape. Drain the beans, discard the Bouquet Garni. Reserve the extra cooking fluid.

The steps up to this point can be done in an InstaPot. Starting with dried beans, add the water and Bouquet Garni, and then follow your manufacturer's suggestion for cooking time. Once done, strain the beans from the cooking liquid and reserve. You can also skip this by starting with canned beans.

For the Cassoulet

2 cups dried beans, cooked until tender *or* two 14 ounce cans of beans, rinsed and strained

6 cups bean stock, or water, or other reserved stock

1 Tbsp. tomato paste

1 Tbsp. chopped garlic

½ cup white wine

3 cups chicken stock (in reserve)

½ cup breadcrumbs

1 Tbsp. chopped fresh parsley

Salt and Pepper, to taste

PLUS

Meats or vegetables as described below

Meats, Traditional cassoulet can be made with a variety of meats; in fact, it makes a great way to use up leftovers. Use a selection of 2-3 meats, or for a vegetarian version, roast some large pieces of root vegetables and winter squash until they have a caramelized golden-brown color. Layer them with the beans as you would with the meat. Meats can include: link sausage, chicken, goose, duck confit, ham, pork belly or bacon (or both?), pork skin, lamb, etc. I made mine with 4 chicken thighs, ½ pound kielbasa, and ½ pound bacon, all from my freezer. The variety and amounts are up to you.

Vegetables. A cassoulet can be a dish of just beans and meat, but I like to add other vegetables as well. I added 3 cups of big chunks of carrot, onion and celery to the cooking grease and sautéed them until they started to get some color.

Directions

Roast meats in a hot oven or sear meats in a frying pan until they start to show some color. Remove from pan, reserve the cooking grease.

Sauté vegetables in reserved cooking grease until golden brown. Add beans and garlic to vegetable blend and toss to coat. Add tomato paste, white wine, and 1 cup of the reserved bean stock. If there is not enough of the bean stock, use chicken or other prepared reserved stock. Allow to cook for a few minutes to combine flavors. Add salt and pepper and season to taste.

In a deep casserole or Dutch oven, begin to layer the meats alternately with the bean and vegetable mixture. Continue until the pan is full. Add enough stock to barely cover.

Bake uncovered at 325 degrees for one hour or until the center of the casserole is bubbling.

Raise oven temp to 400 degrees. Bake for 20-30 minutes until a brown crust has formed on top. With a spoon, break the crust and add more broth to bring the level back up to the top. Add the optional seasoned breadcrumb and parsley mixture as a topping at this point if desired.

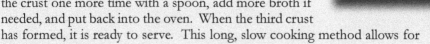

Lower the oven temp to 350 degrees and bake for another 20 minutes or until a second crust has formed. Break the crust one more time with a spoon, add more broth if needed, and put back into the oven. When the third crust has formed, it is ready to serve. This long, slow cooking method allows for rich, deep flavors to develop, and it is worth the time to let it happen!

Remove from the oven and allow to cool for several minutes until it stops bubbling. Serve with some crusty bread and butter, and you have a delicious, hearty meal!

PORK WITH MUSHROOMS IN CREAM SAUCE
Eric Brown - Peachtree Corners, Georgia

Just at the beginning of the Pandemic, but before we were in lock down, friends came over to the house for dinner. We served this with steamed broccoli, my Hymnal salad (see elsewhere) and for dessert, Jamie Oliver's microwave marmalade puddings (think microwave mug cake with soul).

1 ¼ pound pork tenderloin, sliced into 1 ½" cubes	2 Tablespoons butter
1 large onion diced finely	¼ cup sherry
5 ounces sliced mushrooms	1 Tablespoons paprika
8 ounces chicken stock	1 ½ Tablespoons flour
½ cup Crème fraîche	1 ¼ tsp salt
1 Tablespoon oil	¾ tsp pepper
	parsley to garnish

Slice the meat into 1 ½" slices and dry off.

Heat a pan and place in oil and butter, then brown the meat thoroughly. Set the meat aside on a warm plate. Add onion to pan and soften for 2 minutes. Add flour, paprika, salt and pepper and continue to cook for 1 or 2 minutes. Slowly add the cup of chicken stock and ¼ cup of sherry to the mixture and bring to the boil.

Add the meat (and any juices) back to the pan and bring back to the boil.

Lower heat and simmer for 30 to 40 minutes (if you are serving this later in the day, you can stop at this point and then reheat before the meal).

Add the mushrooms and cook for about two minutes, then add the Crème fraiche. Place in a serving dish and top with parsley.

If you don't have Crème fraiche, then you can use sour cream into which you have placed a tablespoon of flour, but absolutely do not let this boil at this point or the sauce might curdle. Serves four.

NO-BOIL CORNED BEEF AND CABBAGE
Heather Mbaye - Carrollton, Georgia

Corned beef (from the grocery, with spice packet)
a head of cabbage
3 Tablespoons of olive oil
salt and pepper (white or black) to taste
*This recipe requires either a slow cooker or
instant pot cooker.*

Corned Beef
Preheat your instant pot on the sauté setting. Open and rinse the corned beef, reserving the spice packet. Once the instant
pot is heated, sear both sides of the corned
beef. If you are using a crock pot, sear the
beef on the stovetop in a cast iron pan or
skillet.

Deglaze the instant pot bottom with
enough water to cover. For most instant
pots, you will need to us about 1 cup of
water. My instant pot is a 10 quart instant
pot, so I use about 2 cups. If you are using
a slow cooker, deglaze your pan or skillet
and reserve the water.

Place the rack into the instant pot and put the corned beef on top. Ensure
the water is NOT touching the meat. You are not boiling the meat, you are
steaming it. If you are using a slow cooker, put the cooker on low – RESIST
THE LURE OF THE HIGH SETTING – and either put a rack in or cut
well washed potatoes in half or quarters to raise the meat out of the water.
Put the water from the deglazed pan into it and place the meat on top. Sprinkle the spice packet on top.

Cook a 2-3 pound corned beef in an instant pot about 1.5 hours. Cook a
2-3 pound roast in a slow cooker on low only for about 10-12 hours. Longer
is better. I know it will be done enough to eat more quickly, but it will be
delicious and fork tender if you are patient. If it doesn't fall apart when you
touch it with a fork, put the top back on and keep cooking it. For goodness
sake, don't boil the meat.

Cabbage
Preheat oven to 350F.

Roughly chop a head of cabbage, avoiding the hard white center stem.

In a large bowl, toss it with 2-3 tablespoons of extra virgin olive oil; salt
and pepper to taste. Roast about 45 minutes or until preferred tenderness
is reached. Serve with corned beef.

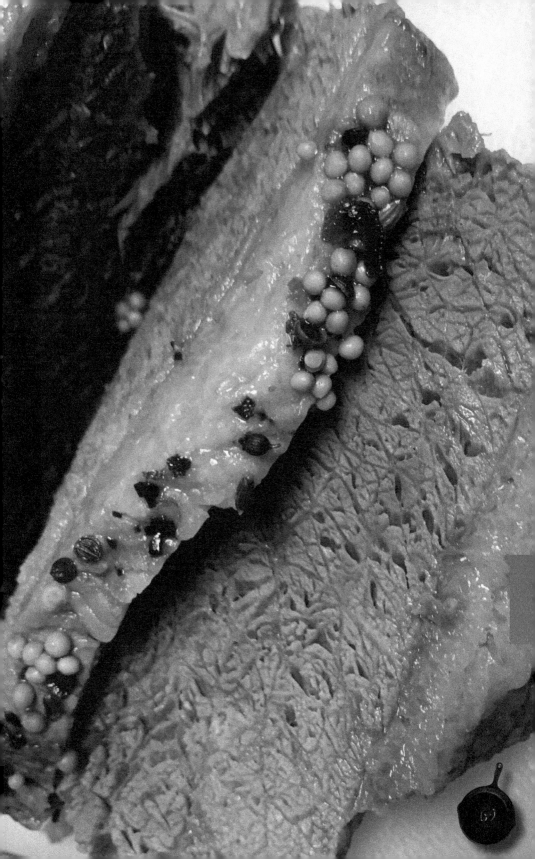

RABBIT AND DUMPLINGS
Jessica Saucier - Little Rock, Arkansas

1 whole rabbit, cleaned and quartered
   (you can substitute 2 squirrels or a chicken)
1 medium onion, diced
2 Tablespoons minced garlic
Salt and pepper
Cavender's Greek Seasoning
3 bay leaves
1 teaspoon celery seed or a couple chopped celery stalks
2 quarts chicken stock or broth (you can make with bullion if need be)
Vegetable oil
3 cups self-rising flour
Milk

In a large stock pot, heat 3 tablespoons of vegetable oil and add diced onion. Season the rabbit with salt, pepper, and Cavender's then dust liberally with flour. When the onion begins to become clear, add the rabbit pieces and fry until brown. Add 1 quart chicken stock, celery seed or chopped celery, the garlic, bay leaves and more Cavender's if desired. Cover and stew rabbit until it begins to fall off the bone. At this point, you can remove and debone the meat or leave it on the bone.

Bring stewed rabbit to a boil, add half the second quart of stock or broth. Add milk to the flour until it makes a slightly sticky dough. Drop in spoon-fulls into the boiling liquid, don't add too many at once. When they float to the top and puff up, they are done. Taste broth to see if it needs additional seasoning and adjust to taste. Serve over steamed or dirty rice.

DIRTY RICE
Jessica Saucier - Little Rock, Arkansas

3 cups raw rice	Salt
½ pound chicken livers	Cavender's Greek Seasoning
1 pound ground beef or pork	Cayenne pepper
1 small onion	1 Tablespoon bacon grease
Garlic powder	Butter

Cook rice until done, but not mushy. While rice is cooking, in a cast iron skillet melt bacon fat and cook onion until clear, add chicken livers and ground beef and as they cook mash the livers up. Season to taste with garlic powder, cayenne, Cavender's and salt. Cook until done.

In a greased 13"x 9" cake pan mix the cooked rice and meat mixture until well blended, taste and adjust seasoning to suit. Top rice with a few pats of butter and bake at 350 F for 20 minutes or until lightly browned on top.

BEEF PIE

Grav Weldon - Little Rock, Arkansas

2 prepared pie crusts	1 12 ounce bag frozen mixed vegetables
2 pounds chuck roast, trimmed	1 Tablespoon flour
2 onions, chopped fine	1/2 cup water
1 Tablespoon Worcestershire sauce	Salt and pepper to taste

In a Crock-Pot, place roast, onions and Worcestershire and cover. Cook over high heat for one hour, then reduce to low until the roast can be shredded with a fork. Add vegetables. Make a slurry with the flour and water and pour into Crock-Pot. Cook over low an additional hour.

Butter a deep pie pan and line with crust. Spoon beef filling into pie pan, then cover with remaining crust. Be sure to vent crust.

Bake at 350 degrees for 50-55 minutes or until crust is golden brown. Remove from stove. Rest 10 minutes before slicing and serving.

HERB CHICKEN POT PIE
Zara Abbasi - Little Rock, Arkansas

2 pie crusts
  (store bought or homemade)
4 to 5 cups shredded chicken
1/2 cup each of chopped onions,
  carrots, and celery (or make
  it easy and buy a store bought
  version of soup starter)
2 Tablespoons garlic paste
2 Tablespoons flour
2 cups heavy cream
4 to 5 sprigs of thyme
1 sprig rosemary
1 bay leaf
2 to 3 sage leaves
1/2 teaspoon each dried oregano and parsley
1/2 package each frozen corn and green peas '
Salt and pepper to taste.
Egg wash for top plus additional ½ tsp each of dried oregano and parsley

Preheat oven to 375 and line one of the pie crusts in a pie pan. Use a fork to make holes in the crust. Set aside.

In a large Dutch oven, add in oil and brown onions, carrots, celery and garlic until light golden brown. Add in all herbs. Add in the shredded chicken and salt and pepper to taste. Let the entire mixture cook for a few minutes.

Sprinkle in the flour and stir. Add in the cream and let the mixture slowly thicken.

Add in the peas and corn and stir. Check for seasonings and add more if necessary. Remove herb stems and bay leaf and let mixture cool slightly.

Add mixture to the pie shell and cover with the other pie crust and decorate as you'd like. Add vents to the top to allow steam to escape. Use egg wash to glaze the top crust and sprinkle top with ½ tsp each of dried oregano and parsley.

Place the pie on a cookie sheet and bake for 45-50 minutes until the crust is browned and cooked through. Allow to cool and enjoy.

QUICK AND EASY FAMILY POT PIE
Stephanie Wilson - Houston, Texas

2 prepared pie crusts
1 can condensed cream of chicken soup
6-12 oz cooked diced chicken
  (canned is okay)
1 can peas and carrots, or a cup or so of
  whatever leftover veggies you have
1 cup cooked rice (leftover is fine)

Put one crust into your pie pan. Combine all other ingredients, season as desired, and pour into the crust. Lay second crust over all and crimp edges, cut small slits to vent steam.

Bake at 350 degrees for about 35 minutes or until crust is browned.

> Storebought pie crust is fine if you don't make your own, but get a good quality crust like Pillsbury. Fighting with a store brand crust is not worth the hassle.

MISS RITA'S HASH AND RICE
Beatris Pollok - Lumberton, Mississippi

2 12-ounce cans corned beef (Libby's)
1 15-ounce can tomato sauce
about ¼ cup water to rinse tomato sauce can
½ 6-ounce can tomato paste
granulated or finely chopped onion (to taste)
granulated or finely chopped garlic (optional)
cooked rice
  recipe can be halved

Heat the corned beef in a 2-quart sauté pan, stirring to break up, and removing fatty/white bits. Add onion (and garlic, if desired) and mix. Add tomato sauce, water (if too thick or to rinse can), and tomato paste. Stir well.

Let simmer until hot through.

Serve over rice. Garlic bread is a nice accompaniment.

PAEDRIC'S START FROM SCRATCH SHRIMP ÉTOUFFÉE

Pat Mullins - College Station, Texas

> This recipe takes a long time to make, because I start with shell-on shrimp and make my own stock. If you are lazy or in a hurry, use peeled shrimp and canned seafood or chicken stock.

Shrimp Stock

Shells from 2 pounds of shrimp
1/2 large onion, chopped
top & bottom from 1 green bell pepper
2 garlic cloves (~1 teaspoon minced)
1 celery stalk, chopped

2 teaspoons Cajun seasoning
  (I recommend Tony Chachere's
  or Slap Ya Mama)
5 bay leaves

Étouffée

2 pounds shrimp, shell on
  (fresh or frozen)
¼ cup butter (or vegetable oil)
Heaping ¼ cup flour
½ large onion, chopped medium
1 bell pepper, chopped medium
1 large celery stalk, chopped medium
4 garlic cloves, (~2 teaspoons minced)

1 pint shrimp stock (see above)
1 Tablespoon Cajun seasoning
1/2 tsp celery seed
1 Tbsp sweet paprika
3 green onions, chopped
Hot sauce to taste
  (I like Tabasco Sauce)

Make the shrimp stock: Pour 2 quarts of water into a pot and add all the shrimp stock ingredients. Bring to a boil, cover, reduce heat, and simmer the stock gently for 45 minutes, stirring occasionally. Strain through a fine-meshed sieve.

You will only need about 2 cups of stock for this recipe. Use some of the left over stock to cook your rice, for added flavor. Whatever is left can be used for soup or other seafood dishes. It will last in the fridge for a week or two, or frozen for up to three months.

Make the roux: To make the Étouffée, start by making a roux. Heat the butter (or vegetable oil) in a heavy pot over medium heat for 1 to 2 minutes. Stir in the flour, making sure there are no clumps. Let this cook, stirring often, until it turns very brown; this should take about 10 minutes or so. DO NOT LET IT STICK.

Add the vegetables: Add the celery, green pepper, and onion, mix well and cook this over medium heat for 4 minutes, stirring occasionally. Add the garlic and cook another 2 minutes.

Slowly add shrimp stock: Measure out 2 cups of the shrimp stock and slowly add it a little at a time, stirring constantly so it incorporates. The roux may absorb the stock and seize up at first, then it will loosen. Add additional stock as needed to make a sauce about the thickness of gravy.

Add the Cajun seasoning, celery seed and paprika and mix well. Add salt to taste, then mix in the shrimp. Cover the pot, turn the heat to its lowest setting and cook for 10 minutes.

Serve over white rice, with cornbread or biscuits. Garnish with green onions, add hot sauce to taste.

SFINCIONE
Margie Raimondo - Little Rock, Arkansas

Dough
About 3 1/2 cups/500 grams flour (all-purpose)
2 1/4 teaspoons (25 grams) active dry yeast, dissolved in 2 Tablespoons
  warm water
1 teaspoon fine sea salt
About 8.5 fluid ounces/250 ml water

Form the flour into a volcano-like shape with a center well on a large wooden cutting board or clean kitchen counter. Add the yeast (dissolved in water) to the center with the salt, and then the water. Knead until the dough is homogenous and form into a ball. Cover with a kitchen towel and let rest for at least 3 hours.

Topping
2 Tablespoons olive oil, plus more for greasing the pan
3 medium onions (thinly sliced)
6 plum tomatoes (ripe, peeled; canned are fine)
2 cloves garlic (peeled and thinly sliced)
6 anchovy fillets, finely chopped
  (you may omit these, if you're allergic or not a fan)
1/2 pound Caciocavallo or Pecorino Romano
1 Tablespoon oregano (chopped fresh or 1 teaspoon dried oregano)
1 ½ cups breadcrumbs (homemade or store-bought)

Heat the olive oil over low heat in a large skillet. Add the sliced onions and sauté until softened and translucent, about 8 to 10 minutes. Add the tomatoes and garlic, using a wooden spoon or spatula to help the tomatoes break down as they cook. Continue cooking until sauce is slightly thickened, another 15 to 20 minutes.

Prepare the Pizza
Preheat the oven to 450 degrees Fahrenheit. Grease a baking sheet with olive oil. Spread the rested dough in a layer in the pan (about 1 inch high). Spread the anchovy pieces evenly over the dough and press in gently. Sprinkle about a quarter of the grated cheese over the crust, then cover evenly with a thin layer of the tomato sauce and sprinkle with the remaining grated cheese, the bread-crumbs,, and the oregano. Drizzle the top generously with more olive oil, and then bake until the cheese is melted and the cheese and breadcrumbs are lightly browned, about 15 minutes. Slice into squares and serve. Can be served hot or at room temperature. Serves 10.

CHICKEN TAGINE
with Dutch Oven option if you don't own a cooking tagine
Heather Mbaye - Carrollton, Georgia

1 pound onions, sliced thin (not cubed)

2 pounds boneless, skinless chicken thighs or breasts (you can use bone-in)

3 Tablespoons total herbal blend, like citrus garlic rub* from Raven's Nest Herbals

1/2 teaspoon mustard powder (optional)

1/2 teaspoon red pepper (optional)

1 teaspoon salt

1 teaspoon white or black pepper

3 Tablespoons total vegetable or olive oil

½ Tablespoon vinegar or lemon juice

3 Russet potatoes** about 2" – 2.5" in diameter and 4-6" long

3 sweet potatoes** about the same size as the russets

8 ounces of fresh Brussels sprouts**

2 small or one large zucchini**

*You can use another rub or spices from your cupboard. This one contains dried garlic, powdered onion, dried and powdered orange peel, dried and powdered lemon peel, black pepper, dried parsley, powdered carrot, and several other ingredients; you can use any combination of herbs and spices you find to be delicious, but make sure you don't skimp!

** The vegetables are mostly up to your choice. What do you have that needs to be cooked? What is tasty for you? However, the onions are NOT optional. They form the base of the cooking and will cook down into almost nothing.

Making the Marinade (all ingredients are already listed above).
Wash chicken and combine it with 2 tablespoons of oil, the lemon juice or vinegar, half the herbal rub, the mustard powder (optional: more or less to taste), the red pepper (optional: more or less to taste), half the salt, and half the pepper in a plastic or glass dish. Do not use a metal bowl as the marinade contains vinegar or lemon, and your meat will pick up a metallic taste that is unpleasant at best and inedible at worst. You should marinate your chicken overnight or all day, but at least two hours.

Cooking

Slice the onions, salt and pepper to taste, and drizzle with some of the remaining oil (about ½ tbsp). Stir to coat.

Slice all the vegetables into spears (sprouts can just be halved). Coat with about half a tbsp of oil and the remaining herbal rub, salt, and pepper (red, black, or white). The potatoes and sweet potatoes can be placed together because they will go in at the same time, but other vegetables should be kept in separate bowls.

Place your tagine (with its heat diffuser) or Dutch oven on the stovetop. Place the onions in the bottom of the dish. Turn the heat on low. Add chicken pieces in a single layer on top of the onions.

Note that a tagine doesn't retain heat as well as the Dutch oven. For comparison, the tagine shouldn't go above 3 on the heat, while the Dutch oven should not go above a 2 on the heat. This is a very slow, steam-heat cooking method.

Cover; cook on low to medium-low for about half an hour, until the chicken is no longer pink on the outside. A low simmer is to be expected, but don't let it boil.

Once the chicken is no longer pink, add the potato and sweet potato spears in a single layer on top of the chicken. If you have on hand other root vegetables, now is the time to put those in.

In about 20 minutes, when the potatoes can be pierced with a knife, add the Brussels sprouts on top in a single layer. After about 10 minutes, again, when the Brussels sprouts are starting to soften, add the squash.

Cook until the vegetables are as soft as you like them. Check the chicken is cooked through.

Serve with couscous or rice, or on its own as a keto-friendly treat!

EASY EGG PASTA IN TEN MINUTES

542 g (3 3/4 cups and 2 Tablespoons) Steve's GF Flour Blend
3 Large eggs (beaten)271 g (1 cup 3 Tablespoons) Water
30 g (2 Tablespoons) extra virgin olive oil
1-2 Tablespoons rice flour for dusting

Place eggs, water, oil and Steve's GF Flour Blend in a bowl fitted for an electric stand mixer. Using the paddle attachment, beat on medium speed for 30 seconds.

Exchange the paddle for the dough hook, then knead the pasta dough at medium speed for 2 minutes until the dough is smooth and comes together.

Remove the dough from the bowl, and placed on a floured surface to knead the pasta into a smooth ball. You can make different pasta shapes with your pasta either by hand, using an extruder or Kitchen-Aid pasta attachment.

To cook the pasta bring 1 quart of water, 3/4 teaspoon salt, and 1 tablespoon of Extra Virgin Olive Oil to a boil. Add pasta and stir occasionally to keep it cooking evenly.

Tip: For al dente – cook 2-3 minutes for fresh pasta depending on the thickness. For dried pasta, cook for approximately 5 minutes.

Tip: Make this great pasta and dry it for meals later in the week. Make any shape you want, then allow the pasta to sit outside, uncovered for a couple hours. You can hang longer noodles on hangers to help keep their shape and allow them to dry.

Tip: Makes wonderful dough for shells or raviolis. Fill with your favorite ingredients and make your favorite shape for a trip to Italy right in your own home!

LEMON THYME RAVIOLI
Ruthie Pepler - Harriet, Arkansas

1 pound ricotta	1 teaspoon garlic powder
1 cup grated Parmesan	1 teaspoon lemon zest
1 egg	2 Tablespoons minced lemon thyme

Mix all the ingredients in a large bowl. Using a tablespoon scoop , drop mounds onto a parchment lined cookie sheet and refrigerate.

Prepare pasta dough and roll out either with a rolling pin or pasta crank to number 4.

Lay out the pasta on a flour dusted board. Place the mounds of cheese mixture onto the pasta about 2" apart. Dip your finger into a small bowl of water and circle around the mound. Lay another sheet over it loosely and press the dough down around the cheese to seal. Dust very lightly with flour. Lay on a parchment lined cookie sheet.

Either freeze or drop into salted boiling water. When they float, reduce gentle boil and cook about five more minutes until tender.

FISKEGRATENG

Eric Brown - Peachtree Corners, Georgia

Syttende Mai (May 17) is Constitution Day in Norway. To celebrate we had Fiskegrateng (poached fish in a set savoury custard), with a salad with orange garlic dressing, boiled carrots, hasselback potatoes and raspberry and blueberry bløtkake for dessert. Some people put macaroni at the bottom of the 9x13 pan and this helps fill out the meal. I don't do this. Also, although we did have this with cod fillets, you can use any fish you want. You can have canned fish, smoked fish, a mixture of fish. You could throw in shrimp if that's to your fancy. Just keep the weight of fish to 500 grams (18 ounces). Makes 6 to 8 portions.

500 grams poached and shredded
   fish fillets (like Cod)
500 ml (2 cups) milk
60 grams (1/2 cup) flour
80 grams (1/3 cup) butter
1 tsp salt

½ teaspoon pepper
1/8 teaspoon nutmeg
3 eggs
¼ cup fresh breadcrumbs (optional)
¼ cup melting cheese (Parmesan,
   Cheddar, Jarlsberg) (optional)

Heat your oven to 350. Grease a 9x13 casserole dish.

Melt the butter with salt, pepper, and nutmeg. Stir in butter and cook for two to three minutes on a medium low heat. You don't want to colour the roux, merely cook out the flour taste. Slowly add the milk to incorporate, but don't bring to a boil. Turn off the heat (and take off the burner if you use an electric hob).

Spread out your flaked poached fish fillets in the bottom of the casserole dish (if you were doing the macaroni thing, enough for six servings of macaroni would go down first, then the fish on top.

Best your three eggs in a bowl and slowly add a few tablespoons of the cream sauce into the eggs to temper them, then whisk this all together. Carefully pour the custard over the fish. If you want, top with breadcrumbs or cheese (I tend to do both)

Bake in the middle of a 350 oven for 35 minutes and then up the temperature to 375 for 10 minutes. You want a golden top. Serve with potatoes and carrots.

PENNE WITH MEAT SAUCE
Joel DiPippa - Little Rock, Arkansas

In the middle of a pandemic with restaurants shut down and social distancing limiting a lot of contact with other people, comfort food is a clarion call. A filling and comforting meal that harkens back to childhood or at least growing up can provide emotional succor as well as physical. For me, the Italian-American staple of pasta with meat sauce is perfect for those times and cravings. Simply put, pasta is ubiquitous in an Italian and Italian-American household and as a growing boy it was also a meal my parents could always provide to me and my brothers.

The Italian-American meat sauce has some similarities to the Italian ragu bolognese but is decidedly a product of American immigrants not only having access to a lot more meat but wanting to make an abundant plate of food to show off how well they have made it. This version builds flavor using both pork and beef, a little bit of wine, and early use of garlic. The penne pasta is a short and tubular shape that will let the crumbled beef in the sauce get into the middle of the pasta but you could use any noodle you like so long as it is thick enough to stand up to this robust sauce

The trick, if there is one, to Italian cooking is to use the best ingredients you can get your hands on and not to mess them up. The Italian way of cooking is about letting the food really speak for itself. I use a local farm to get my meat as part of a community meat share to support the local agricultural community, but you can use whatever the best quality meat you have access to because even the most easily acquired meat will make a great sauce when you are done. Similarly, if you've got local tomatoes to use, try to use them but know you'll probably want to cook the sauce a little bit longer, or add a bit less water towards the end to make up for that. I prefer to use San Marzano tomatoes that are available all year in reputable grocery stores but pay attention as there are many pretenders to the true San Marzano tomatoes but again - use the best option that you have available.

This recipe doesn't really have many tricks or surprises but it is without a doubt one of my favorite meals to make when I need that comfort food fix. Take your time when you are rendering the pork fat, let the beef brown properly, and taste your sauce along the way.

2 cloves garlic, more optional
2 teaspoon red pepper flake or chopped dried Calabrian peppers, less optional
4 ounces bacon or cured pork jowl, diced
½ cup dry white wine, preferably Italian
1 pound ground beef no fattier than 80/20

1 28 ounce can of tomatoes or two pounds fresh tomatoes, optionally peeled
1 pound penne or other dried pasta of choice
olive oil
grated Parmigiano Reggiano (garnish)
chopped Italian flat leaf parsley (garnish)

Equipment

Large pasta pot	Cheese grater
Medium sauce pot	Measuring cups
Wooden spoon	

Set a large pot of water on over high heat to eventually cook your pasta.

In a cool pot, add enough olive oil to coat and the bacon or pork jowl; set to medium high heat. Let the pork fat render out, stirring occasionally, for approximately 2 minutes. The diced bacon should have given up most of its fat, but not be overly crispy yet.

Add the crushed garlic cloves and red pepper flakes to the rendered fat and bacon or jowl bits, reducing the heat to medium. Stir frequently while infusing the fat with the garlic and red pepper flake flavor until fragrant, approximately 3 minutes. Add the ground beef

Add the white wine and deglaze the pan if needed, using a wooden spoon to stir and scrape the bits off the bottom of the pot with the wine, until the wine is reduced by half, approximately 1-2 minutes.

Add the tomatoes, crushing them in your hand as they are added to the pot. Stir to incorporate everything, pressing the big chunks of tomato with the back of the spoon to further break them down and let cook.

When the water comes up to a boil, heavily salt the water and add the pasta. Let the water come to a boil again with the pasta, stirring to prevent it from sticking, and cook until 1-2 minutes short of al dente according to the package instructions. Reserve 1/2C of the sauce while the pasta cooks.

Remove the pasta from the water and add to the sauce while reserving 1/2C or more of the pasta cooking water.

Stir the pasta into the sauce to coat and add 1/4C of the pasta cooking water to add its starch to the sauce and thin it out slightly while the pasta is finishing in the sauce another 2-3 minutes. If the sauce gets too thick or is burning on the bottom of the pot, add more of the pasta cooking water.

Taste the pasta with the sauce to make sure it is properly cooked, and to adjust the seasoning. Tomatoes can take a lot of salt, so if the pasta cooking water didn't add enough salt now is your chance.

Plate your pasta in a shallow bowl using the reserved sauce to make it an overflowing bounty and add the cheese and parsley so that the red, white, and green of the Italian flag shine through.

Mangia! (That means eat up!)

MAC-AND-CHEESE

Grandma Josh Doering - Little Rock, Arkansas

A recipe is not a GPS. A recipe is a road map. It will get you close to where you want to go but not exactly there. Keep this in mind as you cook.

So here's what you do. You've been self isolating for so many damn months, and you're starting to run low.. But! you still have a box of off-brand mac-and-cheese, and some random encased meat. You're good, but you should try to find more foodstuffs tomorrow. For tonight though....

I'm going to assume you've made macaroni and cheese before. After all, you have some right there, so go ahead and start making that. Y'know what? Throw in some Sriracha while that water's boiling. I find it gives a little kick, but isn't as overpowering as if you were just doing straight shots of the stuff.

Next, grab your meat. For the purposes of this recipe, I'm using encased meat to describe a bratwurst, or Italian sausage, or any other dick sized hunk of uncooked ground glory. Go ahead and cut the casing down the middle, lengthwise. Then dig in there and start pinching out little pea-sized hunks of meat and chuck it into the water as it's heating up. (also, the noodles should be in there too. I know the box says to add them to the boiling water, but I've found that just adds unnecessary time.) The flavors and juices and whatnot will intermingle with the 23 cent box of noodles, and encourage them to be better than they are.

When the pasta is cooked to your liking, drain most of the water. Then add the cheese dust. Then eat it and remind yourself to grab more groceries.

PIZZA PASTA
Teresa Horner - Hot Springs, Arkansas

This dish came about after a "make your own pizza night."
I had this and that of toppings left over, so I added a little
extra of some things and came up with Pizza Pasta!
The ingredients below are the toppings we like. If you don't
like some then just leave it out!

8 ounces elbow macaroni noodles (use what ever pasta you have on hand)
24 ounces can of traditional spaghetti sauce (I like Hunts)
1 small can sliced black olives (optional)
2 teaspoon dried Italian seasoning
1/2 bag fried onions ,crushed

Fresh and frozen veggies and herbs

2 cloves of garlic, minced
1/2 sweet yellow onion. diced
1/2 to whole bell pepper (frozen OK)

8 ounces sliced mushroom of
choice (I like portabella)

Dairy

2 Tablespoons butter
2 ounces cottage cheese (Ricotta
cheese if you like)

4 ounces shredded Parmesan cheese
4-8 ounces shredded Mozzarella
cheese

Meats: (optional)

1/2 pound mild Italian sausage,
casing removed and fully cooked
1/4 pound ground beef, fully
cooked

3 slices of lunch deli ham, julienned
1/4 package sliced pepperoni,
julienned
Water as needed

In a deep skillets cook onion, peppers and mushrooms until tender with butter over medium high heat (3-5 minutes). Once tender, add garlic and cook another minute. Add Italian seasoning, olives and sauce along with 1 can of water (use the Hunts can).

Once this comes to a boil, add pasta and meats. Remove from heat and stir in cottage cheese. Transfer mixture to a baking dish that will hold your ingredients (I used 9×13). Bake for 30 minutes.

Once pasta is done to your likeness top with remaining schemes and fried onions. Bake for about 5 -10 more minutes until cheese is melted.

Let set for 5-10 minutes to set then serve.

We liked ours with garlic cheese bread and a simple salad.

87

STACKED ENCHILADAS
Rebecca McGraw - Conway, Arkansas

One thing I learned from hanging out with Deadheads in the mid-90s is that any food can be a burrito if you have a tortilla and the desire to wrap it up. Lately, I've been branching out into making enchiladas out of random things, because almost any food can also be enchiladas if you can spice it right and layer it with tortillas, cheese and sauce. Meat, beans, veg, tofu, whatever. This is great way to clean out the fridge. Do you have a bunch of stuff in there that needs to be eaten and would taste good with salsa and cheese? Well OK then.

We're making stacked enchiladas here because that's the way we, um, don't roll. It's just easier. I've made this three times since mid-March and it's turned out each time as a good way to use up leftover beans and sad vegetables and so forth. There's no need to measure but you do want enough filling to make maybe two or three cups of stuff. In addition to the filling, you need 10-12 corn tortillas (or fewer flour tortillas if that's what you have), a bunch of shredded cheese, and some enchilada sauce or salsa of some sort.

Tonight's filling consists of:
Two sad zucchini from the "crisper"
One sad crookneck squash from same
Half a sad onion
Half a can of leftover refried beans that were in the back of the fridge
 (they're still good, I promise)
Some wilted cilantro
The last little bit of salsa from two jars (one green, one red)
A bunch of cheese

Dice the squash and onion and dump it all in the skilled with some olive oil. Season liberally with taco seasoning and some extra cumin. Dump in the salsa and the refried beans. Leave the heat on low and cook till it's all nice and soft, then spoon into a mixing bowl and dump in a couple handfuls of shredded cheese and the sad cilantro. Taste and adjust seasoning. Stir to combine then let it sit to cool for a bit.

Once the filling is cool enough to work with, build the enchiladas. Take 3 or 4 of your corn tortillas and layer the bottom of the pan. Spread on half the filling. Layer on more tortillas and the rest of the filling. Top with MORE tortillas, then dump enchilada sauce over and sprinkle liberally with more cheese.

Bake at 350° until hot and bubbly. It looks like basic Tex-Mex now, right?

Remove from the oven and note how your kitchen now smells like it needs a margarita. Serve your stacked enchiladas with sour cream and, if you have me, avocado or guacamole. They are also excellent left over the next day, a fried egg on top at breakfast.

Previous incarnations of clean-out-the-fridge enchiladas had fillings of left-over seasoned ground turkey, refried beans, salsa, onions, and diced sweet peppers, with red enchilada sauce, and smushed up baked potatoes, leftover black beans, green chiles, and spinach, with green enchilada sauce. You can really make the filling out of anything as long as it sounds like something that would taste good in a taco and you have enough to make two or three cups of it. I bet sweet potatoes with black beans and green chiles would be good...maybe we'll have that next time. Depends on what we have in the fridge that needs eating.

COMFORT FOOD CASSEROLE
Melinda LaFevers - Searcy, Arkansas

Cook some rice - white, brown, instant, does not matter - your choice, at least enough for four servings, but more may be cooked to stretch the meal for additional people.
Brown up a pound of hamburger.
Drain a can of corn.
Open a can of cream of mushroom soup - two cans if you prefer. Cream of celery and cream of chicken will also work.

When rice and hamburger are both done, mix rice, hamburger, corn, and cream of mushroom soup together. If desired, microwave a couple of minutes to get corn and soup hot, although usually the heat from the rice is enough.

To stretch the meal, use more rice, more corn, and a second can of soup. Other vegetables may be substituted for corn - your taste. A can of chopped mushrooms may be added, if desired, or shredded cheese.

BLACK EYED PEA JAMBALAYA
by Dolores Allemand,
passed to my momma Sally,
passed to me
Sara Puryear-Dunn - Natchitoches, Louisiana

Miss Dolores was from Gonzales, LA. This is one of my go to recipes for Friday night travelers fare, and is super quick. Excellent main dish or side dish.

3/4 stick of butter
1 diced onion (or bag of frozen PictSweet seasoning blend)
1 pound of smoked sausage (or so) sliced into half moons
1 1/4 cup rice
1 can black eyed peas (Trappey's w/bacon is my preference)
1 can of beef broth
1 cup water
I also usually add some garlic powder, thyme and Italian seasoning
Salt and pepper to taste

Melt butter, Sauté onion until tender, add salt, rice, peas, and broth. Stir well. Add water last. Bring to a boil, drop the heat to a simmer, put a lid on it and cook for fifteen minutes, then CHECK. When the rice is done, the dish is done.

If you want to stretch this recipe, add another can of peas and another 1/4 cup of rice and 1/2 cup of water.

Freezes well (so I am told)

CHICKEN SPAGHETTI
Sue Frank - Little Rock, Arkansas

1 roasted chicken cubed
1 1/2 bags frozen mirepoix sautéed
2 small cans mushrooms
1 can mushroom soup
2 cans diced tomatoes
1 8 ounce tomato sauce
Salt and pepper to taste

Cook on low until ingredients are cooked together Remove from heat and stir in 8 ounces grated cheese Cook 12 ounces of spaghetti and mix together

This freezes well.

Desserts

The uncertainty of the coronovirus and how it spread had us second-guessing ourselves a lot, but some things still drew us and others out of our homes. In this case, strawberry season sawed double-thick lines of cars at Holland Bottom Farms in Cabot, where we'd wait over an hour in line for a couple of flats of ripe, perfect strawberries.
Food and flavor became our escape.

EVE'S PUDDING
Suzanne Campbell - Vilonia, Arkansas

For the base
2.5 pounds sliced granny smith apples   ½ cup sugar.

Peel and slice apples place in bottom of square glass dish toss with sugar.

For the cake batter
1 stick butter   2 fresh farm eggs
¾ cup sugar   1 cup self-rising flour
1 teaspoon vanilla   ¼ cup milk

Cream butter and sugar until light and fluffy 3-4 minutes. Add eggs one at a time beat in. Slowly incorporate flour. Add enough milk to make batter fall off spoon slowly. Bake at 350 for 30-40 minutes until golden brown.

Serve with whipped sweetened cream or vanilla ice cream. You can add ¼ cup of blackberries to the apples mixture.

PINEAPPLE BREAD PUDDING
Abigail Eaves - Lakeland Tennessee

One 20-ounce can of chunk pineapple, drained and chopped fine
One whole loaf of sliced bread (white or wheat), cut into one-inch cubes)
Two large eggs, beaten
Half a stick of butter, melted
Three to four cups of milk, scalded (either on the stove or in the micro-
wave); more or less milk to produce a dryer or moister pudding
Half a cup of lemon juice
One cup of sugar
Enthusiastic shake of ground allspice, to taste
Teaspoon vanilla
Half teaspoon salt

Preheat oven to 425 degrees F, and place oven-safe dish of water on bottom
rack. Cut bread and arrange in a large glass baking pan. Scald milk and pour
over the bread.

Mix all other ingredients in a bowl while the bread absorbs the milk. Once
bread has completely absorbed the milk, pour the rest of the ingredients over
the milk/bread and combine in the pan, stirring with a fork.

Bake for 45-60 minutes, until a toothpick comes out clean after being poked
into several places in the pan and the pudding is at desired firmness.

Enjoy as-is or with s scoop of vanilla ice cream.

EMMA HANSON'S WARTIME CARROT PUDDING
Eric Brown - Peachtree Corners, Georgia

During World War Two, sugar and fats were rationed but molasses, fruits and vegetables weren't and fats like suet and margarine were took fewer ration stamps than butter.

2 ounces (60 g or ½ cup) self rising flour
2 ounces (60 g or ½ cup) breadcrumbs (not the dry type from a can, but left over from bread)
1 ounces (30 g or 2 Tablespoons) sugar
1/8 teaspoon salt
½ teaspoon cinnamon
¼ teaspoon nutmeg
¼ teaspoon dried ginger
½ teaspoon cardamom
2 ounces (60 g or 4 Tablespoon) suet or vegetable shortening
2 ounces (60 g or 3 Tablespoon) candied peel (I use dried cranberries instead or chopped up candied cherries)
4 ounces (120 g or ¾ cup) of dried fruits like raisins, golden raisins, dried cherries)
2 ounce (60 g or 1 regular) carrot, grated
2 ounce (60 g or 1 small) raw potato, grated
1 Tablespoon Molasses
1/8 teaspoon baking soda
Orange juice, about ¼ cup

Grease a 1-quart bowl (or if you have a 2 pint pudding basin, great).

Measure all the ingredients and add all of them (except the orange juice), in the order listed, mixing after every addition (you can add all the spice at one time), in a mixing bowl. Add enough orange juice to make a batter of a dropping consistency (not so loose that it pours out, you must drop it in the container).

Drop the batter into the bowl/basin and smooth out the top. Cover loosely with waxed paper (or plastic wrap) and tie this on tightly to the top of the bowl.

Place in a pot with enough simmering water to come half way up the bowl and cover the pot. Simmer for 2 ½ to 3 hours, checking occasionally to see if you need to add more boiling water. I Place it in a slow cooker.

After three hours, remove from water and let sit for 20 minutes before unmolding onto a plate. Serve with custard sauce

You can do this much more quickly in a microwave but, you must first micro-wave all of the dried fruit with ¼ cup of liquid and let it sit for 10 minutes. Then mix everything together in order, making sure that the bowl is micro-wave safe. The cooking time in the microwave will vary, but check at three minutes with a skewer, which should come clean. If not, then microwave in periods of 1 minute until baked.

CUSTARD SAUCE ON A BUDGET

Whisk together an egg yolk with a tablespoon of cornstarch and 1 table-spoon of sugar with a teaspoon of vanilla. Slowly add a half cup of milk and a half cup of cream (or, even all milk or all cream or a cup of half-n-half). Put in microwave for 20 second blasts for the first minute, then 15 second blasts for the second, stirring vigorously between each blast. You are looking for a point where you can run your finger on the backside of a spoon and the line stays there. Immediately cover with plastic wrap touching the top of the sauce (to prevent a skin forming) and cool in refrigerator.

BLACK AND WHITE BREAD PUDDING

Kat Robinson - Little Rock, Arkansas

1 gallon bread chunks, one inch in size
  (can be sliced bread, croissants,
  doughnuts, baguettes, or buns)
2 cups milk
6 eggs
1 cup sugar

1 teaspoon salt
1 1/3 cups white chocolate chips,
  divided
1 1/3 cups dark chocolate chips,
  divided

Pre-heat oven to 350 degrees. Grease a pan – a 9"x13" pan works fine. So does a divide lasagna pan. Or a Bundt pan. Be creative.

Beat eggs. Add sugar and salt and incorporate. Whisk eggs together with milk.

Pour milk and egg mixture over bread chunks. With your clean or gloved hands, gently work the bread into the liquid. You don't want to mush it into a homogeneous putty, rather you want to still be able to make out inch sized lumps of bread. Just make sure everything gets a bit wet.

Divide mixture in half. Add one cup white chocolate chips to one half and one cup dark chocolate chips to the other half. Pour in the white chocolate mixture and pat flat. Pour over the dark chocolate mixture and pat flat.

Place in oven and bake 40-50 minute, or until the mixture no longer giggles wetly in the pan. The edge will form a crust. If you are using a deep but narrow vessel for cooking, it may take longer and you may want to cover the top to prevent over-browning.

Remove bread pudding from oven and invert over cooling rack. It won't look fabulous, but you have a solution for that.

After 15 minutes, you may place the entire bread pudding on a platter or slice it and lay it out on a tray. If you choose to serve it immediately, warm is for the best. If not, you can warm it in a 225 degree oven for 15 minutes before serving.

In a small glass measuring cup, place remaining white chocolate chips and microwave in 15 second increments until melted. Drizzle over bread pudding. Repeat with dark chocolate bread pudding. Enjoy.

STEAMED CARROT AND GINGER PUDDING

Eric Brown - Peachtree Corners, Georgia

125 g self-rising flour (this is a little under a cup)

Zest and juice of 1 lemon

100 grams grated carrot (this is a large carrot or about 1 ¼ cups)

100 grams chopped candied ginger (If you didn't have this what you could do is chop up dried apricots or use golden raisins, and plump up in some ginger ale mixed with ginger powder…in other words, make this your own pudding)

50 grams ginger past (this is about 2 Tablespoons of the stuff you can get in a tube. If you have fresh ginger, 19 grams of ginger root and 31 grams of water and blitz in a blender.

½ cup of soft butter (115 g)

127 grams of brown sugar (about 1 ¾ cups)

4 eggs (3 extra large eggs)

½ teaspoon pumpkin pie spice

1/8 teaspoon dried coriander (don't have, don't worry)

Cream the butter and sugar together. Add one egg at a time, then the juice and zest of the lemon, incorporating it all. Sift all the dry ingredients together and then into the creamed mixture and beat on medium for a minute. Fold in all the other ingredients. Place in a 1.7 litre pudding basin that has been well greased and into which a small circle of parchment paper has been placed on top. Cover with plastic wrap and steam for 1 ¾ hours. Allow to cool in the basin for a couple of hours before serving. Serve with any custard sauce, but the fancy tea and ginger flavoured custard sauce is smashing with this.

FANCY TEA AND GINGER FLAVOURED CUSTARD SAUCE

Warm up 5 fluid ounces of milk (150 ml) to steaming point and the put in two teabags and 1/8 teaspoon of cardamom and 5 grams of fresh ginger (or ¾ teaspoon of ground) and let steep for 10 minutes. Strain this into 8 ounces (250 ml) of cream. Meanwhile take three egg yolks, three tablespoons and 1 teaspoon of sugar and 1 teaspoons of cornstarch and whisk together, slowly adding the milky cream mixture. Put in microwave for 20 second blasts for the first minute, then 15 second blasts for the second, stirring vigorously between each blast. You are looking for a point where you can run your finger on the backside of a spoon and the line stays there. Immediately cover with plastic wrap touching the top of the sauce (to prevent a skin forming) and cool in refrigerator.

AMARETTO CAKE
Gigi Coulson - New Orleans, Louisiana

For the cake:

3 cups all-purpose flour
2 3/4 cup sugar
1 cup whole milk
2 sticks unsalted butter, softened
4 large eggs
1 Tablespoon white vinegar

1/2 teaspoon baking soda
1/2 teaspoon salt
1 Tablespoon vanilla extract
2 teaspoons almond extract
1/4 cup amaretto

Set your oven to 325°F and preheat. Grease a Bundt-style pan.

In a bowl, stir your milk and vinegar together briskly. In another bowl, combine your baking soda, salt, and flour with a whisk.

In a large mixing bowl cream the butter and sugar until fluffy. Then beat eggs in one at a time. Stir in both extracts. Add in the flour mixture using a hand mixture alternating it with the milk and amaretto.

Pour your batter into the bundt pan. Bake for 60 minutes at 325°F. Allow cake to cool before removing from the bundt pan.

For the Amaretto glaze:

1 stick unsalted butter
1/2 cup packed light brown sugar
1/2 cup sugar

1/3 cup half and half
3 Tablespoons amaretto

For the glaze: combine sugars and butter in a sauce pan over medium heat
until smooth. Add amaretto and cream, then bring to a simmer while stir-
for five minutes. Remove from heat and let cool. Serve the cake drizzled
the amaretto glaze. YUM.

CHOCOLATE BROWNIE CAKE
Robert Welch - Kansas City, Missouri

1 stick of butter
4 Tablespoons cocoa
1/2 cup shortening
1 cup water
1/2 cup milk
1 1/2 Tablespoons vinegar
2 eggs
1 teaspoon baking soda
1 teaspoon vanilla extract
1 1/2 teaspoons cinnamon

In a large bowl, mix flour & sugar. In a medium bowl, mix eggs, baking soda, vanilla & cinnamon.

Melt in a saucepan the butter, cocoa, shortening, and water. Sour the milk with the vinegar. Add saucepan's contents and milk to the egg mixture. Pour the liquid over the flour mixture. Mix well.

Pour the batter into a 17" x 13" sheet cake pan (cookie sheet). Bake at 375°F for 20 minutes.

Icing:

1/2 stick (4 Tablespoons) of butter
6 Tablespoons milk
2 squares baking chocolate

1 pound powdered sugar
2 teaspoons vanilla extract

Slowly melt butter & chocolate in milk. Mix in the powdered sugar. Pour over the cake while both cake & frosting are still warm. This should create a thin smooth glazing over the top of the cake.

CARROT CAKE
Susannah Austin - Memphis, Tennessee

Matty let it slip the other day that he liked things like zucchini bread and carrot cake. He's even requested a carrot cake made with carrots and zucchini for his birthday,

Started with a boxed cake mix... carrot cake with carrot flavored pieces. It called for 2/3 cup of oil, 3 eggs, and 1 cup of water.

I did that, but switched out 2/3 cup of milk for the 1 cup of water, since I knew the added vegetables would add more moisture.

Then, because I can't find my shredder, I spiralized two carrots and a zucchini, and took the scissors to it.

Mixed all that together, and poured it in a bundt pan for baking.

Bake at 350°F for 41-46 minutes.

Just took it out of the oven, and let me tell you, it smells amazing. I'm letting it cool in the pan for a while, first... Then I'll flip it, and let it finish cooling on the rack, itself.

SOUR CREAM COFFEE CAKE

Amy Harvey - Kansas City, Missouri

1 cup margarine	1 teaspoon vanilla
2 cups sugar	2 cups cake flour
2 eggs	1 teaspoon baking soda
1 cup sour cream	1/2 teaspoon salt

Cream together margarine and sugar. Add eggs and beat well. Mix together sour cream and vanilla and fold it in. Mix together flour, baking powder and salt and mix into sour cream mixture by hand. Pour into greased and floured 8x12 or 9x13 pan.

Topping:

1 cup chopped pecans	6 Tablespoons brown sugar
2-3 teaspoons cinnamon	3 Tablespoons butter
2 Tablespoons sugar	

Mix all ingredients well and spread over batter before baking.

Bake 40 minutes at 350 degrees until lightly browned.

GLUTEN FREE PUMPKIN MUFFINS WITH PUMPKIN PURÉE

Ruthie Pepler - Harriet, Arkansas

1 stick unsalted butter at room temp
1 3/4 cups (spooned and leveled)
   Steve's Cake Flour
1 1/2 tsp baking powder
1/2 teaspoon baking soda
1/2 teaspoon salt
1 1/4 cups pumpkin purée

1 cup sugar
3/4 cup buttermilk
3 large eggs
2 teaspoons vanilla
2 teaspoons cinnamon
1/4 teaspoon ground ginger
1/4 teaspoon nutmeg

Whisk all dry ingredients together except sugar.

Beat butter and sugar together until light and fluffy. Add eggs and vanilla
Stir in dry ingredients, then add pumpkin and buttermilk. Beat on medium
until just smooth

Preheat oven to 350'. Scoop out batter into lined muffin tin, making sure to
completely fill the cups. Let stand in pan until oven is heated.

Bake 30-35 minutes. Test for moist crumb on toothpick

BUTTERMILK GLAZE

1 cup confectioners sugar   Up to 1/4 buttermilk

Pour sugar in a bowl Slowly add 1 tablespoon buttermilk at a time. Stir
between each tablespoonful until glaze reaches desired consistency.

GLUTEN FREE PUMPKIN MUFFINS WITH PIE FILLING

Ruthie Pepler - Harriet, Arkansas

1 stick unsalted butter at room
  temperature
1 3/4 cups (spooned and leveled)
  Steve's Cake Flour
1 1/2 teaspoon baking powder
1/2 teaspoon baking soda
1/2 teaspoon salt

1 can pumpkin pie filling
1/2 cup sugar
3/4 cup buttermilk
3 large eggs
2 teaspoon vanilla
1 teaspoon cinnamon

Whisk all dry ingredients together except sugar.

Beat butter and sugar together until light and fluffy. Add eggs and vanilla. Stir in dry ingredients, then add in pumpkin and buttermilk Beat on medium until just smooth.

Preheat oven to 350 degrees. Scoop out batter into lined muffin tin. Be sure to fill the cups. Let stand until oven is heated.

Bake 30-35 minutes. Test for moist crumb on toothpick.

CINNAMON & BROWN SUGAR PUMPKIN PIE
Zzavvalynn Anderson - North Little Rock, Arkansas

1 ½ cup canned pumpkin

1 cup brown sugar

1 Tablespoon ground cinnamon

1 teaspoon ground nutmeg

½ teaspoon ground allspice

3 eggs, beaten

1 cup evaporated milk

1 unbaked 9 inch deep dish pie shell

Combine pumpkin, brown sugar, cinnamon, nutmeg, and allspice. Add eggs amd mix well. Gradually mix in evaporated milk. Pour into pie crust.

Bake 425 degrees for 15 minutes. Reduce heat to 350 and bake an additional 35 - 45 minutes. Cool. Serve plain, with whipped cream, or with vanilla ice cream

COUNTRY COBBLER
Sara Puryear-Dunn - Natchitoches, Louisiana

This recipe was handed down to me by my mother,
Sally McCrary Puryear.

First, dump a bag of frozen fruit in a bowl and let it thaw for about an hour.
It should give you about two cups. I usually cut the frozen sliced peaches into
hunks once thawed. If using fresh fruit, you need two cups of fruit. A little
more does not cause problems.

Crust

Stick of butter (1/2 cup) melted   Cup of self-rising flour
Cup of white sugar   3/4 cup of milk

Stir gently. Dump into a 8x8 glass casserole dish.

Add 1/2 to 3/4 cup of sugar to the fruit, depending on the sweetness desired. Dump on top of the batter.

Cook in a 375 degree oven for 40-50 minutes. If the edges are browning too
fast, cover with foil strips.

Options:
- If using all purpose flour, add 1 1/2 teaspoon baking soda and 1/2 tea-
  spoon salt.
- With apples, add cinnamon, all spice, and nutmeg to the batter. Season
  apples with brown sugar instead of white sugar
- Apples seem to make the crust more like cake to me. Still yummy.
- I added lemon juice into my blueberries last night, two tablespoons or so.
  I usually add a dash of nutmeg to the batter with blueberries or peaches.

PANTRY PACKET OATMEAL COOKIES

Kelli Marks - Little Rock, Arkansas

This is a very easy recipe for the kids, using those instant oatmeal packets to make the perfect breakfast cookie.

1/4 cup (4 Tablespoons) butter, melted
1/4 cup brown sugar
1 cup flour
1/4 teaspoon salt
1/2 teaspoon baking soda
1/2 teaspoon baking powder

1 egg
1 packet of your favorite instant
    oatmeal (any flavor will do)
1/4 teaspoon cinnamon (optional)
Raisins, dried fruit, nuts (optional)
Cinnamon and sugar mix

Preheat oven to 350 degrees.

Mix everything in a bowl with a spatula. Roll balls about 1.5 inches thick with your hands, then dip into mix of cinnamon and sugar and place separately onto lined cookie sheet. Lightly smash.

Bake for 10 minutes at 350 degrees.

Yields 6-8 cookies.

FRESH STRAWBERRY POPSICLES

Zara Abassi
- Little Rock, Arkansas

2 cups fresh strawberries
1/4 to 1/2 cup sugar
Popsicle sticks

Remove stems and cube strawberries. Taste. Add sugar to taste. Let sit a bit to let the sugar incorporate.

Pour strawberries and all juice into popsicle molds. Place top on molds and insert sticks 3/4 way into molds. Place in freezer. Popsicles are ready when they are completely frozen.

BOMBOLONI (ITALIAN DOUGHNUTS)
Margie Raimondo - Little Rock, Arkansas

250g (2 cups) bread flour
250g (2 cups) all-purpose flour
75g (heaping cup) cane sugar
100g (7 Tablespoons) unsalted
   butter, at room temperature
1 package (7g) dry instant yeast
7g (1½ teaspoons) salt

150g (3) whole large eggs
40g (2) egg yolks
110g (1/2 cup) lukewarm water
zest of 1 orange
1 teaspoon vanilla extract
coarse sugar, for coating

Dissolve yeast in lukewarm water, and allow it to sit until it blooms. (very important).

In the bowl of a stand mixer fitted with a dough hook, combine all ingredients except for one of the whole eggs, and beat on medium speed for 5 minutes, then high speed for 5 more minutes. Add in the remaining egg, and beat on medium speed until a smooth and elastic dough forms {you may have to add a little more flour if it seems too sticky}.

Knead by hand for a couple of minutes, then place the dough in a large, lightly oiled bowl, cover with plastic wrap, and allow to rise in a warm place for at least 2 hours until tripled in size.

After the first rise, lightly knead the dough, roll it out to 1.5 cm/0.5 inch thickness, and cut out rounds. Transfer all your rounds to baking sheets lined with wax paper, spray lightly with water, and cover with plastic wrap or a tea towel. Allow the bomboloni to rise another hour and a half until they triple in size once more.

When ready to fry, heat oil in a large, deep pan to a temperature between 170-180C (~350F). Fry the bomboloni without crowding the pan. Fry them for about 3 minutes on each side, until they are golden brown, then drain off the excess oil, and set them on a wire rack to cool. While they are still warm, pour some granulated sugar in a small bowl, and roll the bomboloni around until completely coated in the sugar. Fill with crema or chocolate. Makes 20.

Crema

250ml milk
15g granulated sugar (for the milk)
1/2 vanilla bean
2 egg yolks
45g granulated sugar (for the yolks)
18g cornstarch

15g unsalted butter
3g gelatin (1.5 sheets)
Whipped cream
150ml heavy cream (cold, with
   30%-35% fat)

Soften the gelatin in cold water for 10 minutes. Heat the milk with half of the sugar and the vanilla bean in a saucepan.

In a bowl, whisk together the egg yolks, sugar and corn starch. When the milk is boiling, pour it in three times over the egg mixture through a strainer and mix every time to prevent the yolks from curdling.

Put back the liquid mixture into the saucepan and cook on medium heat, whisking continuously. Allow the pastry cream to boil for 2 minutes then remove from the heat, add the diced butter and whisk again until it is fully incorporated.

Squeeze and add the softened gelatin to the pastry cream. Pour the hot pastry cream in a large container. Cover the pastry cream with plastic wrap and store in the fridge.

RECIPE BY CONTRIBUTOR

INDEX

Books by Kat Robinson

Arkansas Pie: A Delicious Slice of the Natural State
History Press, 2012

Classic Eateries of the Ozark and Arkansas River Valley
History Press, 2013

Classic Eateries of the Arkansas Delta
History Press, 2014

Another Slice of Arkansas Pie: A Guide to the Best Restaurants, Bakeries, Truck Stops and Food Trucks for Delectable Bites in The Natural State
Tonti Press, 2018

Arkansas Food: The A to Z of Eating in The Natural State
Tonti Press, 2018

101 Things to Eat in Arkansas Before You Die
Tonti Press, 2019

102 More Things to Eat in Arkansas Before You Die
Tonti Press, 2019

Coming Fall 2020
A Bite of Arkansas: A Cookbook of Natural State Delights

These remaining pages are provided
for your own recipes.

CPSIA information can be obtained
at www.ICGtesting.com
Printed in the USA
LVHW022009291020
670162LV00009B/322